Nonviolence: Origins and Outcomes

3rd Edition

Nonviolence: Origins and Outcomes

3rd Edition

Charles E. Collyer and Ira G. Zepp, Jr.

TryForFurther Books
Uniontown MD

Nonviolence: Origins and Outcomes, 3rd ed.
Part 1 - *Discovering Nonviolence*
Part 2 - *Agape and Ahimsa: Twin Roots of Nonviolence*

ISBN-13: 978-1978395886
ISBN-10: 1978395884

Cover Painting " River Run Harmonies"
by Ellen Elmes.
Image prepared by Don Elmes

Dedications

For John Lidgey, 1948 - 2001, my friend of 50 years,
who was intensely interested in nonviolent change.
In grateful memory,
- Charlie

For Montgomery J. Shroyer - Biblical scholar,
social activist, nonviolence teacher.
With gratitude and respect.
- Ira

Acknowledgments

I will always be grateful for the opportunity to work with Ira Zepp during the last decade of his life. Ira had a way of being both reassuring and challenging at the same time — what a friend! As we explored the overlap between his field of religious studies and mine, psychology, I experienced both the joy of an interdisciplinary collaboration and the vertigo of stepping out into unknown territory. In the end, he became a pretty good psychologist, and I came to appreciate the insights into nonviolence that have arisen in many of the world's religions and in the thinking of many theologians.

As always, I thank my wife and partner Pam Zappardino, who first introduced me to her mentor Ira Zepp many years ago, and who continues to guide our work together through the Ira and Mary Zepp Center for Nonviolence and Peace Education.

I also thank the people of Common Ground on the Hill, Silver Oak Academy, Shepherd's Staff, NAACP Branch 7014, and all the other members of my community who provide me every day with nonviolent discoveries and wonderful examples of *agape* and *ahimsa* in practice.

Charles E. Collyer
Carroll County, Maryland, 2017

Contents

Preface to the Third Edition

The late Dr. Zepp and I have been gratified by how our students and friends have responded to the first two editions of *Nonviolence: Origins and Outcomes*. The book has been read as a text in courses and discussed in book clubs, and has even been reported useful as affirmation and inspiration, although that goes a bit beyond its original purpose.

Nonviolence: Origins and Outcomes grew out of my experiences as a teacher of psychology and Dr. Zepp's as a teacher of religious studies and theology. Each of us in our own way was learning how to teach about nonviolence, a subject that both of us felt must be "brought down to earth" if its lessons were ever to take strong root.

The first edition, published in 2003, was written with the events of September 11, 2001 fresh in our minds. The second edition (2007) made the book more widely available beyond the United States and India, as the use of the book in schools and colleges began to grow. In this third edition, the entire book has been revised and updated, it has been split into two volumes, titled *Discovering Nonviolence* and *Agape and Ahimsa,* and it has migrated to electronic form. *Discovering Nonviolence* (comprising five of the original chapters) is an introduction to nonviolence, viewed as a comprehensive moral and practical framework for solving problems. *Agape and Ahimsa* (comprising four of the original chapters), represents Ira Zepp's thoughtful analysis of the philosophical

12

and religious roots of nonviolence, including a dialogue with Bill Holmes about pacifism.

Two chapters are also available as separate ebooks. The first, *What Goes on in a Nonviolence Training*, will be of interest to trainers and teachers of nonviolence, and to intermediate and advanced students. The second, *There's More to Nonviolence Than I Thought,* amplifies the commonplace saying that nonviolence is active rather than passive, by discussing several specific ways in which a person may be changed when considering nonviolence more deeply.

Charles E. Collyer
Carroll County, Maryland, 2017

Foreword to Nonviolence: Origins and Outcomes

The past century has brought humankind into an era of mass destruction, one where our ability to produce massive suffering seems to have raced ahead of our capacity to demonstrate compassion for one another. We must search for paths into the future that will turn away from destructive goals and strategies, paths that will reject violence as a way to solve problems. If we are to rise to a new level, it will be necessary for us to re-examine basic concepts, re-draw our roadmap, re-direct our footsteps, and re-shape our vision for the future.

This book by Charles Collyer and Ira Zepp makes a significant contribution to the field of nonviolence and peace studies. The experience of the authors as teachers of nonviolence, and the depth of their commitment to nonviolent social change, is evident in every chapter. Many scholars and practitioners will benefit greatly from this work, particularly those who have recently come into this field of study and are developing their own skills as teachers of peace. This book lays out a foundation of *ahimsa*, *agape* love, and achievable nonviolence that belongs in the forefront of the 21st century's search for a new way.

Dr. Bernard LaFayette, Jr.

Part I. Discovering Nonviolence

Prologue: An Unplanned Experiment

It was mid-January, the beginning of a Spring semester at the University of Rhode Island. I was then Chair of the Psychology Department, and the instructor for a group of first-year graduate students in the department's orientation seminar. These students were impressive. All had come to the university with strong credentials. They displayed an obvious enthusiasm for learning more about Psychology, and held high expectations of their program faculty. Most were in their mid-twenties to mid-thirties, some coming directly from bachelor's degree programs and some from the working world. They were not kids, but grown men and women with at least a semester of graduate work under their belts, well-educated and pretty sophisticated.

The roster consisted of about twenty students from our three program tracks - Clinical, Experimental, and School Psychology, all mixed together. This integration was more the exception than the rule in their courses, because for the most part the three programs functioned separately. In this seminar, however, the students were getting to know each other during their first year, and learning about the department's faculty, its research resources, and the current state of the field of Psychology.

We were meeting on a Monday. The Martin Luther King Jr. Holiday was coming up the following week, so our second seminar meeting of the new semester would be in two weeks' time, and I made an announcement to that effect. Then, having mentioned the holiday, I happened to ask how many people had ever read Dr. King's *Letter from Birmingham Jail*. No one raised a hand.

I had become a nonviolence trainer about two years before. In that role, I had often assigned the *Letter* and led discussions on it. But my nonviolence workshops usually consisted of younger students or members of community groups. I had never assigned King's *Letter* to graduate students in Psychology.

Still, I was surprised that no one in this well-educated group had read the *Letter from Birmingham Jail*. I asked how many people had ever read anything by Dr. King. Only a couple of hands were raised. One person related that when she was in high school, her class had spent a day learning about the Civil Rights Movement. She knew Dr. King mainly for his "I Have a Dream" speech, which she remembered reading. She was hazy on the details of what had happened during the Movement. She had heard that I was involved in nonviolence training, and that the curriculum I used was derived from King and Gandhi. She reflected that that her brief high school exposure to the Civil Rights Movement had not included a discussion of nonviolence, or King's relationship to it.

I decided that this was one of those "teachable moments" when a gap has been acknowledged and the next step would be to fill it in. I said something like this: "Well, I'm going to give you an assignment. Go out and find something to read by Dr. King. It can be the *Letter from Birmingham Jail*, or anything else. When we get back together in two weeks, we can talk about what you found. I'm especially interested in what you think about King as a psychologist." (Without meaning to, I left open the question whether "as a psychologist" meant "the psychologist," placing King in the role, or "from a psychological viewpoint," inviting the student to be the psychologist. Consequently, some people interpreted the assignment one way, and some the other way.)

That homework assignment turned out to be one of the most successful I have ever given to a group of students, at any level. When the class met again two weeks later, almost all were genuinely excited about King and nonviolence and civil rights and the psychology of it all. They had located and read King's *Letter*, and many other books, sermons, and essays. Several expressed amazement that they had not known of King as a thinker and writer before this. Some had decided to participate in one of the King holiday events because of the assignment. The students were full of admiration for King's moral approach to difficult conflicts, for his ability to respect and even care for his adversaries, for his skill as a coalition-builder. And they were fascinated by the dynamics of nonviolence, by its counterintuitive yet very natural quality, and by its power at times to cut through human problems and provide surprising solutions. The relevance of nonviolence for psychology, and vice versa, just leapt out at them. One student asked, quite early in our discussion, "Why didn't I ever have a course on this?" Indeed.

On that day I began to wonder why Psychology and the traditions of nonviolence were not in closer touch with each other. Because the historical origins of nonviolence lay outside the relatively young field of Psychology, in other disciplines such as religion, politics, and literature, and in social problems outside the academy, it was understandable that the topic had not made its way into the standard curricula of Psychology programs. But the impact of nonviolence in practice, and its influence on people's thinking and emotions, loudly say "psychology" to me, and I have come to believe that a stronger bridge needs to be built between the two domains.

Nonviolence grew originally from religious roots. Psychology is a secular, not a religious, field of study. Yet many psychologists readily acknowledge that some "spiritual" understanding of life is important to them, and that though they find spirituality largely missing from the mainstream of their field, they feel it is an important element in their own work and in understanding human nature. Martin Luther King, Jr. And Mahatma Gandhi before him, each crafted a practical social vision of his religion, combining a positive, spiritually satisfying view of humankind with political energy for progress toward freedom and justice. Psychologists join with many other audiences in finding that such a combination of spirituality and practicality fills a void for them.

This book has been written to whet an appetite for nonviolence in as many readers as possible. We think it will appeal to both students of "official" Psychology, and to people interested in everyday psychology who also have an interest in spiritual and social values. More generally, we believe that nonviolence offers "common ground" where religious and secular concerns can intersect, and where bridges can be built between cultures, disciplines, and factions of many kinds. We have seen the study and practice of nonviolence reap rich and creative rewards, and so wish to encourage as many people as possible to explore this common ground, to begin the building and crossing of these bridges.

Chapter 1 - Discovering Nonviolence

Before digging into the stories and the conceptual richness of nonviolence, most potential students of the topic seem to hold a stereotype about it - a set of four beliefs that, by default, capture the meaning of the word "nonviolence" for them. First is the belief that nonviolence is a passive philosophical approach in which events are just allowed to happen without any intervention or interference. Second, a person may associate nonviolence with cowardice, and violence with courage. Third is the idea that nonviolence is just being nice to people. And fourth is the view of nonviolence as being easy, as being the path of least resistance in many of life's challenging situations.

A little study soon shows that nonviolence is the very opposite in every respect. It involves active problem solving rather than passive acquiescence. It very often requires awesome courage in the face of real threats and terrible fear. It is likely to demand difficult confrontations, and intense discomfort both for the just and the unjust. And it has therefore been the more difficult path, the road less traveled, in almost all of its most famous examples. These contrasts, and others, help to explain why the discovery of nonviolence very often involves a series of surprises for the new student.

Why does the old stereotype of nonviolence persist? Many reasons could be given, but it seems to us that the understanding of nonviolence as passive, cowardly, "nice", and easy, is maintained by very strong psychological and cultural forces. Further, some of these forces are accepted and familiar, but upon reflection just don't make sense. Others are hard to perceive, much less to challenge. We will discuss some of these forces in this chapter and throughout the book.

Despite these forces, nonviolence continues to be discovered, and rediscovered, by people who need it. Throughout history, in many cultures all over the world, people have discovered the power of nonviolent motives, feelings, tactics, and values. Nonviolence has given direction to religions, enabled embattled peoples to survive, and achieved dramatic triumphs over injustice and violence.[1] However, the understanding of nonviolence as a powerful antidote to both violence and complacency is often lost, or submerged in a culture's repertoire of traditions, and so must be explicitly rediscovered again in response to a new set of problems.

Between rediscoveries, when people have slid into the acceptance and even glorification of violence, and when wealth and distance enable many people to evade basic human problems rather than solve them, the stereotyped view of nonviolence - passive, cowardly, nice, easy - prevails. The stereotype is abetted by the structure of the word nonviolence itself: "nonviolence" sounds like it should simply mean "not violent," a phrase with apparently obvious passive connotations.

Possessing this understanding of nonviolence, people paradoxically both approve of it and are frightened and confused by it. They endorse it as a remedy for the violence that frightens or annoys them, and are enthusiastic about its adoption – at least by others. However, they confidently "know" that they themselves could not stick with nonviolence if their own lives or family were threatened. They proclaim that nonviolence will not work in situations that have reached crisis proportions.

Well, to address the last point first, sometimes nonviolence has worked in crisis situations. But for some reason we do not tell stories about the courageous and successful use of nonviolence very often. Perhaps nonviolence is just as frightening to us as violence! Perhaps we believe that we will be made vulnerable if we embrace nonviolence, as if we were not already so. Perhaps we refrain from telling stories about nonviolence to protect ourselves, and our loved ones, from exposure to danger.

But what if telling stories of nonviolence were more likely to help us survive than to put us in danger? It would then be tragic if we did not tell these stories and try to learn from them. We will tell some of the stories of nonviolence in this book, and you can judge their value for yourself. Some of the stories are indeed about crisis situations, but many are about how crises can be prevented through a nonviolent approach to life and its problems.

Quitting Smoking and Learning to Swim

Here are two analogies that may capture the idea of nonviolence as a skill set or a life-long practice rather than a temporary tactic or momentary decision.

Quitting smoking is never seriously suggested as a cure for the person who is already dying of cancer. Rather, we understand that quitting, if done early enough, can reduce a person's risk of getting lung cancer in the first place. We would not test the value of "quitting smoking" by its failure to cure a terminally ill person. Yet nonviolence is often put to such a test, when it is finally tried as a form of eleventh-hour crisis intervention. Nonviolence is often deemed to have failed when, in a crisis, it does not magically make the threat of violence go away. This kind of test is unfair; it is like dismissing the value of quitting smoking because a critically ill recent quitter died anyway. Why would people reject nonviolence so unfairly? Perhaps this is one of the ways in which we human beings defend ourselves against the supposed dangers of adopting nonviolence. "See? We tried nonviolence, and it didn't work." (That is, it didn't magically overcome violence *right now*.) "So now, let's go back to our old habits."

A second meaningful comparison is to swimming. Learning nonviolence is very much like learning to swim. Like swimming, nonviolence is enriching, useful in everyday tasks, preventive of threats to life, and very helpful when threats nevertheless arise. Everyone understands the value of swimming lessons. However, not everyone understands the value, or has even heard of, systematic lessons in nonviolence. It is important to know that during the U.S. Civil Rights Movement and in other human rights movements around the world, nonviolence training was undertaken to prepare for predictable threats such as being beaten up or attacked by police dogs. Demonstrators in the campaigns where nonviolence was the guiding principle were not thrown unprepared into the sea of injustice and hostility, but received lessons ahead of time that taught them what to expect and how to respond. We will see later that it was their adherence to what they had learned in those lessons that made it possible for the movement to strike down legalized segregation.

The phrase "sink or swim" brings to mind the limited, frightening options of an unprepared person floundering in crisis. Sometimes this phrase is adopted literally, as a strategy for teaching someone how to swim; in that case it means plunging the student into deep water on the first day of the course. We leave to others the task of judging the merits and shortcomings of this approach to learning. However, we are pretty sure that mastery cannot be achieved in this way. That is, we are confident that regardless of how one was introduced to the water, it is best to take progressively more challenging lessons, get lots of practice, and master the skills of swimming well before a real crisis arises when floundering simply will not do. The same can be said for many other skills, including the skills of nonviolence.

If we are lucky, crises occupy only a small fraction of our lives. Nonviolence may or may not provide the solution during the 1% (say) of our days when we are in real crisis. But it certainly provides valuable guidance during the other 99%. In fact, it might be said that all the problems successfully solved in this larger portion of our time, are examples of nonviolence at work. Should we not study our own successes in order to learn how to have more of them? In this book, we will present nonviolence as something to practice not just when the threat of violence is about to overwhelm us, but all the time. We believe that this more comprehensive approach is in keeping with what Mahatma Gandhi and Martin Luther King Jr. meant by nonviolence.

The Meaning of Nonviolence

We have said that the old stereotype of nonviolence is mistaken, and that the structure of the word itself gives a wrong impression of what nonviolence means. Naturally enough, nonviolence does include opposition to violence. One of the origins of nonviolence discussed in our *Agape and Ahimsa: Twin Roots of Nonviolence*, is *ahimsa*, the Sanskrit word meaning non-injury, a vow not to commit violence in any way. Nonviolence also means valuing and caring about human beings, simply because they are people. Accordingly, the other root of nonviolence is *agape*, the Greek word for unconditional love toward others. In addition to these two roots, the meaning of nonviolence resides in the lives of people who are trying to follow a nonviolent path, and in the nonviolent solutions they create to address life's problems. So for us, the meaning of nonviolence has come to include both its origins, *agape* and *ahimsa*, and its outcomes as expressed in nonviolent living and problem-solving.

As you can see, nonviolence for us is not a simple idea but many-faceted, not a single idea but a constellation of many. Throughout history, many versions of nonviolence have developed, some from religious traditions and some with more secular or combined roots. We adopt an inclusive "big tent" approach in which all of these versions are valued, and are seen as tending in the same general direction. We do not presume to speak for them all, but we will try to refrain from elevating one specific version over another. Can a general, "big tent" definition of nonviolence be given? Perhaps not to everyone's satisfaction, given this complicated picture, but here is an attempt:

Nonviolence is an approach to life in which people are valued for their own sake, and in which the idea of successful living includes peace achieved through peaceful means. It demands the best that

people have to offer, both in crisis situations and in the course of everyday life. It is active, courageous, realistic, and challenging. It can be learned. Nonviolence does not have to be performed perfectly. But to the extent that it can be practiced, it makes a valuable contribution to the quality of life and to relationships between people, whether they are friends or adversaries, by creating conditions that support human beings rather than doing violence to them.

Obstacles and Paradoxes

We hope that nonviolence sounds interesting and attractive so far. It has been so attractive to some of our students that they have asked us for advice on how to make a career out of teaching nonviolence. A few of them have actually done so. It turns out, however, that advocating for nonviolence on a large scale is quite difficult. For many people in society today, significant obstacles stand in the way of adopting nonviolence. In our opinion, there is a pressing need for more understanding of these barriers to nonviolence education and for more people who are willing to work on overcoming them. Here are just a few of the obstacles we have encountered in our work:

First, everyone in the world seems to believe that the world would be better off if only *everyone else* were less violent. Now, if everyone endorses nonviolence at least to this extent, why is the world still so violent? Clearly, we need to come to terms, not only with the violence of others, but also with our own. Ironically, most of us have a strong, even desperate, tendency to cling to violence as an option for ourselves, and to avoid serious consideration of living without this option.

Second, the wisdom of the ages regarding violence and the feelings associated with it, is sometimes not so wise. For example, the idea that anger must be cathartically "vented" is very widespread. In fact, many people believe that when angry, greater harm will come to them if they take some time to think about how to respond than if they act out their anger immediately. However, decades of research, less widely known, support the alternative views that (1) the perceived necessity of venting anger is just a compelling illusion, and (2) learning skills to deal with anger is more effective in almost every way. For a readable treatment of alternative theories of anger, see Carol Tavris's book *Anger: The Misunderstood Emotion*.[2]

Third, when the wisdom of the ages really is wise, we sometimes just don't get it. An example is the Golden Rule: Treat others as you want them to treat you. For the most part, this is a profoundly good, nonviolent insight.[3] Too often, however, we operate on what might be called the Rule of Payback: Treat others the way they have treated you. This rule is also expressed in the familiar saying: An eye for an eye and a tooth for a tooth. Some people apparently cannot distinguish between the Golden Rule and the Rule of Payback; they just don't get the difference. Justice is equated, not with fair and respectful treatment for all, but with getting revenge; and peace is equated, not with positive, constructive lives and relationships, but with simply being left alone.

Fourth, we human beings become adapted to unjust and destructive conditons all too readily. What is *familiar* to us through long experience - even if the experience is ghastly -

comes to feel *normal* through mere exposure and repetition. And violence is usually repetitive. Most of the violence in the world occurs in repeated cycles of payback for the most recent outrage from our enemies, which in turn was justified by them as a response to our own attacks, and so on and so on. With a moment's reflection, it is clear that a great deal of the world's violence could be prevented if people could stop these cycles. But we are acccustomed to these cycles, because the pattern is repetitive. We tell ourselves that this is normal, natural, the way things have always been. Some even object to nonviolence as abnormal and unnatural, perhaps because they are so unfamiliar with it.

Fifth, although violence and hostility are real threats to everyone, we do not often teach the ideas and methods of nonviolence. We could teach them if we chose to do so; the knowledge is available. However, to propose that nonviolence be taught in schools is very controversial in many communities. In some places the objection is that it is not an academic subject. In others nonviolence is greeted with the suspicion that it is religion, or that it is politically slanted. Other communities will claim that they do not need it, even as bullying goes on in school hallways and among students on the internet, teenage drivers (in imitation of their elders) succumb to road rage, and badly handled emotions lead to partner abuse, battering, and rape.

This list of obstacles could be extended, but already it provides a glimpse of what could be called resistance to nonviolence: a complex of barriers and paradoxical elements in human life, which prevent us from taking greater advantage of nonviolence to live more successfully. The good news is that when we come to understand these barriers, their power lessens, and we can then overcome and move beyond them.

Welcomed Nonetheless

Resistance to nonviolence is based on some real fears and concerns, which teachers of nonviolence should acknowledge. When people's feelings of vulnerability and need for security are respected, the rich and inclusive version of nonviolence that we are talking about here will be welcomed by most audiences.

Nonviolence is perhaps most warmly welcomed in communities where violence is overt and prevalent. Although people may carry the old stereotype of nonviolence with them when they come in for a workshop or presentation, and although their initial response may be slightly cynical or suspicious, audiences usually recognize quickly that "this nonviolence stuff" is important knowledge to have. A teacher often senses that there is a widespread hunger for the ideas and skills of nonviolence, a hunger which most schools and other institutions apparently do little to satisfy.

Is Nonviolence Applicable to All Levels of Conflict?

As a working hypothesis, we will claim that the basic ideas of nonviolence are applicable all the way from the individual and interpersonal levels of human life and problem solving, up to the societal and global levels.

These levels have certain features in common. For one thing, every intentional act of violence, from the individual to the international, seems to possess a compelling rationale in the mind of at least one human being. Here are some examples: One man was only trying to "teach my wife a lesson" when he beat her up. Another said he had no choice, because the other guy at the bar had given him "the look." A young woman felt justified in slapping her child because the kid just wouldn't shut up, even after she had yelled at him. A general ordered his troops to destroy a village in retaliation for a sniper attack, and called in air support to eliminate an enemy gun position. In a talk on just-war theory, a national security advisor attempted to summarize the conditions under which it is rational and proper to wage war. This advisor had given similar speeches about three recent wars, finding in each case that the conditions for a just war had been satisfied.

Are there similar brain pathways involved in the experience of felt necessity and justification in all of these cases? We suspect the answer is yes. Cognition and emotion are quite important for understanding what is going on before, during, and after violence.[4] If we learn that a person committed an act of violence, we can be fairly sure that the person perceived (correctly or mistakenly) that he or she had been threatened, disrespected, or harmed by somebody else. Or they may have been afraid that they were about to lose power and control over someone like a spouse or partner, or a vital resource such as oil. There was almost certainly a personal logic, in the mind of the violent actor, that rationalized his or her violence. James Gilligan has argued that almost all violent actors have previously experienced intense shame, or personal disrespect, and so believe that they are acting out of justifiable self-defense, self-protection, or self-assertion.[5]

Another aspect of violence that seems to run the gamut of levels, from personal conflicts to wars, is a tendency by the agents of violence to discount the "collateral damage" caused by their behavior. Violence causes both intentional effects (harm done that the violent actor meant to cause) and incidental effects (harm done that was not intended). Collateral damage is a euphemism for the incidental, unintended destruction of violence, but the labels "collateral" and "incidental" are cruelly meaningless to the people who are harmed. Effects are effects. There is no law of nature saying that the intended effects of violence will be the only significant ones, the most lasting, the most remembered, or the only ones for which the initiators of the violence will be held responsible. In fact, damage that one party regards as "collateral" may very well become the reason in another's mind for the next round of retaliation.

The subjectivity and arbitrariness of what is called collateral damage are greatly under-appreciated by violent people. The main thing on a typical violent person's mind, at the time of the violence, is a highly personal fantasy about control, revenge, punishment, destruction, or "winning." The imagined consequences of the violence make up a distorted cartoon, in which the enemy is eliminated or neutralized, and the problem of the moment is therefore solved. It never turns out to be as surgically effective in real life as it was in the violent person's mind; there are always messy collateral consequences, every bit as real as any intentional damage that was inflicted. But at the time of the violence, these downstream consequences are conveniently minimized in the mind of the violent actor. One of the factors that undermines the credibility of "just war" claims is that the cost-benefit calculations that ostensibly precede a decision to wage war, are inevitably rigged by this discounting of the costs of collateral damage.[6]

We claim that nonviolence has important things to teach us about these and other problems, which range from individual problem-solving to the global level. We do acknowledge that the difficulties in applying nonviolence are significant and daunting. However, one advantage of adopting a broadly inclusive vision of nonviolence is that the full range of human creativity and potential for constructive problem-solving can then be brought to bear.

How Much Nonviolence Do We Need to Learn?

Even a small dose of nonviolence education can affect a person's thinking about conflict and the options available for dealing with it. Chapter 2 contains several reaction papers written by students who had simply viewed two short documentaries about the use of nonviolence, one a story from India about Gandhi, and the other an episode about the sit-ins that were part of the American Civil Rights Movement. The two stories combined took less than an hour to watch, and they are available online if you would like to reenact what the students did. However, just reading Chapter 2 will give you a fascinating glimpse into the range of constructive thought sparked by these two examples of nonviolence.

Systematic training is a higher dose of education than watching videos, and yields more profound effects. But what does nonviolence training involve? Chapter 3 outlines a version of nonviolence training in the King tradition, explaining what is covered in a typical two-day workshop, and how. We think the logic of the training will make sense to you, but that you will nevertheless encounter some surprises. For one thing, the range of topics covered in the workshop may be wider than you thought it would be.

Chapter 4 attempts to convey some sense of the expanded view of nonviolence, and of the world and life itself, that many people gain from experiencing such a training and from further study of nonviolence.

Chapter 5 addresses the task of making nonviolence real, in two ways. First, research that has evaluated the effectiveness of nonviolence is briefly reviewed; and second, the application of nonviolence in police work and the military is described.

We have developed and delivered nonviolence education programs for people of all ages, from many backgrounds and in many walks of life. Therefore the language used here is deliberately secular, although it can be adapted to the needs of almost any group. The companion volume, *Agape and Ahimsa: Twin Roots of Nonviolence*, complements this book by discussing the historical origins of nonviolence in Christianity and in Hinduism, and may be especially appropriate for use in religious settings.

If you are new to nonviolence, we hope these books will open up the topic for you, and leave you eager to learn more. If you are already familiar with one or more of the traditions of nonviolence, we hope that our presentation of these ideas will provide a valuable new slant on this fascinating, vitally important, and inherently interdisciplinary and multicultural field of study.

Chapter 2 - What Students Learned From Two Nonviolent Movements

Although nonviolence is not a traditional school subject, and although most students in the United States receive almost no instruction in it, it is remarkable that even a brief exposure to nonviolence elicits strong feelings, and quick recognition that it is important.

The student reaction papers in this chapter were written by students in a General Psychology class at the University of Rhode Island's College of Continuing Education in Providence. The students were diverse in age, racial and ethnic identification, and gender. The course introduced Psychology by presenting five general perspectives on the field, of which one was termed the Sociocultural.[7] Within the Sociocultural part of the course, topics such as prejudice and stereotypes, power and social influence, cultural identity, and group processes were discussed.

One morning, the class viewed two segments from the Public Broadcasting series on nonviolence movements, *A Force More Powerful*.[8] The first documentary focused on the 1960 Nashville sit-in movement, in which our colleague and friend Bernard LaFayette Jr. had been one of the student leaders. The second documentary was about the 1930 Salt March led by Mohandas Gandhi in India. Students were asked to write a short reaction paper on what they had seen.

The scope of each documentary will be described next, and then the students will take over with their reactions.

The Two Movements

Nashville, 1960

There are many nonviolent movements from around the world that are now available for study.[9] The one chosen by the producers of *A Force More Powerful* to represent the U.S. civil rights struggle was the Nashville sit-in and boycott campaign of 1960. The sit-ins in Greenville North Carolina, Nashville Tennessee, and subsequently in many other communities, stand as an intermediate phase between the early events of the Civil Rights Movement such as the Montgomery bus boycott, and the later campaigns such as Birmingham and Selma, which changed federal laws. It has been argued that the Nashville campaign convinced Martin Luther King Jr. to place renewed emphasis on nonviolent direct action, and so set the stage for the campaigns of the mid-1960s that produced the Civil Rights Act of 1964 and the Voting Rights Act of 1965. David Halberstam has recounted the story of the Nashville movement and its impact in some detail, in his book *The Children*.[10]

In the winter of 1959-60, Diane Nash, Bernard LaFayette Jr., John Lewis, James Bevel, and other students at Nashville colleges began to attend evening workshops on nonviolence let by Rev. James Lawson. Martin Luther King Jr. had asked Lawson to come south from Ohio to teach Gandhian methods to young people interested in challenging the Jim Crow system of racial segregation. In the workshops,

Lawson's young friends learned about the term *ahimsa*, and Lawson connected it to the Christian ideal of love, *agape*. They discussed the successes of nonviolent campaigns under Gandhi's leadership in India, and earlier in South Africa. They debated how to respond to threats and intimidation nonviolently, without impulsively provoking an escalation of violence. They practiced sitting quietly in rows while their friends role-played white bigots who taunted and even physically attacked them.

The students organized a strategy for desegregating lunch counters in several downtown department stores, by having groups of black and white students sit down together and order food. They were refused service as a matter of store policy, because the stores at that time could discriminate against black customers. The white reaction to the sit-ins progressed during the first weeks of the campaign from amazed inaction to semi-organized resistance. Groups of young white men attacked the students, as had been anticipated in the workshops. The demonstrators, following their training, did not retaliate. However, they were arrested and jailed, while their attackers were not charged - a contrast that was soon noted. The nonviolent strategy increasingly drew national attention to the cause of desegregation, and stimulated open questioning of Nashville's official stance on what was legally allowed in the city and what was not.

After a bomb blast destroyed the house of Z. Alexander Looby, the students' legal counsel, there was a march to City Hall, which received a high level of media attention. Diane Nash confronted Ben West, the mayor of Nashville, with the question whether it was right for stores to discriminate against some of their customers on the basis of their color. With the cameras running, the mayor declared that it was not right. This dramatic declaration was the beginning of a process that desegregated Nashville's businesses and other public facilities once and for all.

This successful nonviolence campaign deserves to be more widely known. The video segment from A Force More Powerful is a very good introduction to this piece of American history.

After viewing the Nashville documentary, the students watched another half-hour video about Mohandas K. Gandhi, the person whose work earlier in the 20th century had inspired Lawson and provided a model for the Nashville demonstrations.

India, 1930

Gandhi's two careers were long and rather complicated. He became known as a proponent and leader of nonviolent social change during his first career as an attorney in South Africa. After returning to his native India in 1915, his second career was devoted to moving India toward independence from British colonial rule. *A Force More Powerful* provides succinct glimpses into the two careers. The introduction to the series begins in a South African jail, and notes not only Gandhi's contribution to the early struggles for human rights in that country, but also his influence on many nonviolent movements of the 20th Century which were to follow. The documentary we watched focused on the Salt March, providing a visually compelling illustration of Gandhi's methods and an overview of the struggle for Indian independence.

In March of 1930 Gandhi, by now a revered nonviolent "saint" throughout much of India, chose the British tax on salt as the target of a direct action campaign. Britain enforced a monopoly on the manufacture of salt in India, and imposed a sales tax on it. Salt was a relatively minor part of the overall economy of the British Raj, but the impact of the salt tax was felt by everyone, and especially the very poor. Furthermore, as a symbol of unreasonable exploitation, the salt tax could be understood to represent a much wider array of grievances. The campaign was initiated by marching 240 miles from Ahmedabad to Dandi, on the seacoast, where salt would be made for free in defiance of the British law.

In several ways, the Salt March exemplified Gandhi's approach to noncooperation with unjust systems. It focused on a specific issue, the salt tax, rather than everything at once. It entailed discipline and planning; his core group of marchers were members of his own ashram, who understood nonviolence and the purpose of the demonstration. It was extended over a period of time to allow attention to be drawn to the issue; at about 10 miles per day, it took many days to walk 240 miles. It provided opportunities for many people to participate in very simple ways; a supporter of the march could participate by illegally evaporating sea water to recover the salt.

As the documentary makes clear, the Salt March and other actions of the campaign against the salt tax did not immediately produce a dramatic change in India's status. But they set the stage for later political developments leading to independence, and they provided mythic stories that helped Indians to know their own power and to appreciate nonviolence as an instrument of change.

India and Pakistan have had a turbulent history since their independence in 1947 from the old British Raj, and their partition at that time into two countries (now three; the nation of Bangladesh is the former East Pakistan.) However, a feeling of pride in the cultural legacy of Gandhi's nonviolence remains strong; the prevailing view is that Gandhi now belongs to the world, but his home, and the origins of his thinking, remain India.

The Reaction Papers

These short student papers are reactions, not to a full course or workshop on nonviolence, but to less than an hour of exposure to stories that emphasize nonviolent approaches to social change. The views of the students sometimes support the points we have made about nonviolence in other chapters of this book, and sometimes advance contrary ideas or associate the documentaries with other stories and concepts that were meaningful to the individual writers. The reaction papers, from 12 of the 30 students in the class, were selected for their conceptual diversity and for how clearly the writer's ideas were expressed. We particularly invite readers of this book who are teachers to reflect on this sampling of initial thoughts on nonviolence. We have done only minor editing (principally spelling corrections) of the students' writing; we felt that the flavor and meaning of the original papers came through best if we let them speak for themselves as much as possible. However, we did add the subtitles.

The students' stories are intrinsically compelling, but may be even more so if the reader takes an hour to see what the students saw in class. We recommend viewing the two documentaries from the series *A Force More Powerful*. The title of the Nashville story is *We Were Warriors*. The title of the Salt March story is simply *India*.

Disbelief

My reaction to these two films is very easy for me to write about. First, I cannot believe that I did not learn about this in high school. I feel like this is an injustice to me. When I left class last Wednesday, I felt like I wanted to know more about these two movements in history. These movements give such an important message to people. Dedication and teamwork can make anything happen!

The Jim Lawson workshops were awesome. The message was so clear that a nonviolent approach actually meant fighting back. Fighting with nonviolence may seem like more of a challenge, but it is the way people are won over. The way they sat-in every Saturday in the diners, even though they were being beaten over it is such an inspiration. They knew that their arrests dramatized their grievances in a positive way, so it was worth every bit of agony for them. They had to deal with a mayor who claimed to uphold the law but supported the store owners (and men who broke the law by assaulting the students). They were addressing the country and the world with these acts. The progress they made, although it took about three years, was astonishing. Their perseverance is so uplifting. It is good knowing that if something in this world needs to be done, we can do it. We just need to stick together and make people aware.

I was so interested in Mahatma Gandhi. He really was a saint. His way of communicating to the people how and why they were going to be free was very clever. How did he even know that if they made their own salt and clothes, the British would be less powerful? And most importantly, how would one guy get 350 million Indians free from the powerful British government? Because Gandhi was a nonviolent warrior, he won over many people. The government did lose control, because of violence. When police became brutal to Indians, the British civilians began not following the government so strongly. Their violence backfired on them. Although Gandhi was arrested and was eventually assassinated, his work was not in vain. Everything cannot change at once, but Gandhi definitely made something huge happen.

- R. C.

Anger

Viewing the film on non-violent demonstrations and peace, my main reaction is anger. I feel as if the Southern blacks did not have a choice. If they had reacted violently the results would have most likely been death, or jail. Blacks were not given the opportunity to express themselves, the laws were designed against them, and they did not have many advocates. To resort to violence would have probably increased the odds against them.

I am trying to understand the thoughts and actions of the Southern white people. The people seemed unaware of the degradation and horror that must have surrounded these people at this time. To put in place laws that did not allow human beings to utilize even the basic necessities like a bathroom, to me is just not rational. To deny children equal education and opportunity is sinful. The action of these people is a clear contradiction of their professed Christianity.

The idea of non-violence appeals to me in this ins, only because it worked. The Southern blacks achieved wha they set out to achieve, but I imagine myself in the same situation and the anger is overwhelming. I feel the whites should have been beaten and segregated and denied certain rights. I would like to see what the outcome would have been. I do not believe white people would have resorted to a nonviolent protest. I do not believe that they would have the staying power that the blacks demonstrated.

I believe it took intelligence and will for the blacks to carry out an act of non-violence, but my anger is not allowing me to see the psychology in what they did. I cannot speak for all people of color, but if I were to guess, I would say that the majority would have reacted to non-violence with violence.

- C. R.

The Sympathy of Bystanders

The movie we watched in class was very interesting. The students in Nashville used the same method of nonviolence that Gandhi used to bring attention and change to the society they lived in. The approach of nonviolence was very effective. When Gandhi used this approach to get rid of British rule it made the officers look real evil and mean hearted. The reason is looking at footage of police officers beating people in the street looks terrible because the people are not fighting back. It makes a person wonder "How can somebody beat a man or woman for no reason and the person they are beating is not fighting back?" It makes an observer want to listen to the side of the person who is getting beaten because it makes the other side look like savages. That is why

Gandhi received a lot of press from all over, even in America. The same goes for people in the South.

This approach of nonviolence worked when the people in Nashville and the people in India were organized, had a leader, and were consistent. I'm sure if people were not organized with a leader the Indian people wouldn't have gotten their freedom and African Americans would not have gotten the equality they wanted in the South. If only some people followed the nonviolence approach and others did not, things would not have changed in the British Empire or America because if the people who felt they were being oppressed fought back with fists and guns they would have looked like rebels and it would have made the things they were fighting for really nonexistent. The nonviolence approach is a weapon that affects the way a person or people see a situation and when people in Nashville and all across America saw what was going on it brought about change in the South, and the same goes for India.

Another thing I thought about while watching the movie was the nonviolence approach does not just involve the two oppositions but has a third part which is the observer or observers. An example of this is a real life one. I used to go to Classical High School, and I used to go to Kennedy Plaza to wait for buses with my friends sometimes and there used to be a lot of fights there. One time there was a fight where it was approximately four on five. And the kids were going at it, each one throwing wild punches at each other with yelling and screaming. After the fight was broken up you could hear some people saying things like "Well, there kids go again fighting downtown," and "I swear kids love fighting in Kennedy Plaza!" Another time I was downtown there was another fight in which two kids got jumped by three kids. The three kids who jumped them were swinging at the two kids hard, but the only thing the two kids did was cover themselves for protection against the blows until the fight was stopped. They did not throw one punch and even after the fight they did not yell in anger, just looked in disbelief. After the fight some people actually went up to the kids to see if they were all right. Now if you compare these two different instances you can see how the nonviolence approach affects people. In the first case, all of the kids were fighting and the people watching were looking at it like "oh well, there's fighting again." In the second case where the two kids who were getting jumped did not fight back, some people came to them to see if they were all right. So in conclusion somehow the nonviolence approach affects people watching the situation, bringing out their compassion and concern about what is going on.

- P. H.

Closer and Closer to Home

Last week in class we watched a movie titled "A Force More Powerful." This film was about nonviolence and how people today and in the past have changed the world through nonviolence. The term nonviolence is defined as the fight to win someone over without using violence. This film held a very powerful message that I think everyone has to think about and apply it in his or her life.

The first historical event using nonviolence was in Nashville, Tennessee, in 1960. A group was formed to try to desegregate the town's lunchrooms and have everyone dine together. They set out on a Saturday morning by having blacks sit at the diner counters for hours trying to get served. The groups were eventually arrested but had other groups fill in for them directly afterwards. This sent the town into an uproar, no one was injured right away, and eventually it worked. I thought that during this time in history a challenge like this was very courageous. Though the challenge used nonviolence, the lawyer representing the black students had his house bombed. It seems like no matter what technique is used violence is always present in some form or another. Though it is awful to say, sometimes it may seem like the only way.

The true inspiration for nonviolence in America was Gandhi, who set out on a nonviolent task thirty years prior to the sit-ins in Tennessee. Gandhi walked to the beaches of India, setting out to make his own salt and not pay tax, emphasizing injustice to the poor. Though these types of historic leaders are practicing civil disobedience, they are not physically harming people to get their point across. Today it seems no one thinks in these terms. I am personally a large supporter of nonviolence and feel anything can get solved by using this technique. Though I can honestly say I experience violence almost day to day. Whether it is seeing a parent scold a child the wrong way, disrespecting peers or witnessing a fight at a bar, it is all around us. I really thought this film showed a positive message that everyone should learn about in large cities and rural areas.

I come from a small town in Western Massachusetts and in high school there were two groups that were always fighting with each other. I'm sure that if they talked it out they would realize they have a lot in common and that words can get distorted and lead to violence. I thought this video offered a lot of positive information and it really made me think about my personal experiences.

- E. T.

Unthinking Ways

In the movies that we watched in class the one on Gandhi really opened my eyes about what we as a people need to do to overcome all our fears of other races and religions. If there was a force out there that could make all of the races on earth come together and force them to talk about their differences, this would show all of the people that we can all get along together without violence. This would also show people that everybody has the same fears about others, and finally break down the barrier of ignorance. The movies also showed me that the best way to beat an unfair system is to do it nonviolently. This way they cannot make excuses for beating people up or throwing them in jail. The movie showed me that most people don't even think for themselves, they just do what people tell them to do because they don't know how to think on their own. They didn't stop and think that African Americans are people too who have feelings. When Diane Nash asked the mayor if it was fair how African Americans were being treated, he had to stop and think about that question, and finally he said it was not fair. This is an example of how people don't think about the consequences of their actions because they never had to. The South was run like that for years, and after a few generations it becomes a system that everybody follows blindly.

One of the strong points in the movie was when Gandhi started to walk to the ocean and make salt illegally. He picked up a lot of people on the way that felt the same way he did about their oppressors. They felt this way because they were being taxed on something that they needed; they couldn't get around paying for salt because the Viceroy made all the laws and would have them thrown in jail. This is another example of people not caring for another group of people; the Viceroy didn't think of the Indian people as equals, but as second-class citizens or less. If someone had made the Viceroy think about what he was doing or questioned whether the British were there in India for any good reason, it would have made a lot of difference. Perhaps he would have opened his eyes and questioned the point of treating people unfairly. This brings up the point I stated earlier about most people don't even think for themselves. Stanley Milgram's experiment on obedience is related to this.[11]

- A. S.

Bravery and Gratitude

I did not know that Gandhi invented the nonviolence protest tactic. Gandhi's idea was a remarkable beginning to a new era of freedom, not only for his country of India, but for other countries around the world. His protest walk to the salt beach seemed like a small accomplishment at first, but as news of Gandhi's march got around to other communities, more and more people joined his walk for freedom against Great Britain. Regardless of the serious consequences Great Britain placed upon Gandhi and his followers, they continued on with the protest. Gandhi's cause was for the freedom of the Indian people. By believing in this cause, Gandhi knew that he might die because of it. For Gandhi, this was all worth it. Forty years later Americans did the same thing. Black Americans were tired and upset with the segregation between blacks and whites in their community. The African Americans started the civil rights movement against segregated businesses, schools, and jobs in their communities. I agree 100% with this cause and respect every person who was involved with the civil rights movement. I thank all of these brave heroes for my freedom that I have today.

The death and abuse that the African American men, women, and children experienced was so sad. To think that people can be so cruel to humans because of their race! Today, America has come a long way from the 1960s, but America still needs repair work when it comes to fairness between races. Dr. Martin Luther King Jr., Gandhi, and other civil rights leaders and protesters, served a great purpose for the freedom that we have in the world today. We as the new generation must continue the nonviolent fight for rights and peace for all races around the world.

- J. R.

Perspective

After seeing the two documentaries last week, a lot of things were put into perspective for me. I had no idea how bad things seemed to get back then and what lengths were gone through to make things change. I completely congratulate every single person involved in the "lunch room sit-ins." What a great idea to make known that no one was going to stop them from getting the respect that was very obviously deserved. Those students who did that must have had some outrageous courage to do just a little of what they did. They had to know that they had the chance of getting beat, hurt, and even possibly killed just to get their points across to everyone else.

Being white, I am ashamed of all the white people who attacked those black students just for sitting at their "all white counters." Who were they to decide who could and could not sit there? They were not and never would be God, so that was never up to them. Just the fact that those students were arrested for sitting at a counter was horrible in my eyes. What did they do wrong? All they were doing was fighting for the rights that they, as humans, deserved and were not getting. Gandhi was obviously a great inspiration to those students as well as to all of the other millions of people who go along with the "nonviolence" idea. I personally think that this should be enforced all the time. Just looking at what happened here proves that though it may take time, it is possible to win battles by using brains over force and brutality. Is that a hard concept to grasp or what? Obviously, it must be, because though things have changed a lot, things will never be the way they should be. Every single person in this country, in the world, should have the rights they deserve. Being in the U.S. means a person has rights and shall be treated as an equal. Nowhere in that sentence does it say except for color. We need to enforce that, and not be so mean to people just because they aren't white. Color means nothing, brains mean everything. I really like what Gandhi stood for and believe what he fought for and taught his followers were right.

- A. P.

The World Is One

Conflict is everywhere. Sixteen year olds are blowing themselves up in the name of God. Countries threaten each other with trade embargoes and increasing oil costs. Everyone wants it her/his way or no way at all and if anyone disagrees they will be conquered or destroyed. We disrespect our environment; we disrespect each other; and we disrespect that which is greater than ourselves. The world has forgotten that it is one and it must be shared. It has forgotten that boundaries and borders are defined because the human race has deemed it so.

The film on nonviolence presented in class last week showed us how influential leaders of the past avoided violence while fueling major social movements. People such as Mohandas Gandhi and Martin Luther King Jr. were not willing to accept the injustices of the world and expressed their discontent through nonviolent action. I believe many people are equally discontented with society in the 21st century as Gandhi and King were in the 20th. Yet we continuously overlook the importance of nonviolent action. People are showing their anger through fighting and nothing is changing except the increasing amount of violence in the world.

Furthermore, we have become so consumed with individual gain that it has created a great deal of isolationism; for it is much easier to stay in one's own little world than to see the world of one's fellow human being. We must cease inconsiderateness and gradually begin to decrease the level of ignorance we have of one another's lifestyles. A small adjustment in an individual's life, such as using public transportation or walking as often as possible, is a nonviolent action that leads to a decrease in oil consumption which then leads to decreasing the power of oil moguls; a slight decrease but a decrease nonetheless.

Nonviolent action is crucial to making us realize that the world is one and it must be shared as equally as humanly possible. Humanity can decrease violent conflict. We just need to show that we care through what we buy, eat, and drive. The world will shift slowly but effectively. Our choices must clarify that we reject violence and no longer fear peace.

- J. P.

Worth Fighting For

To begin with, I have to say that this video on nonviolence truly inspired me. There are not too many people these days that will stand up for what is right in order to make a change. Rather, every day you hear the world complain about what should be done in order to create justice and equality. Personally, I feel that it takes courage and strength to stand up for what you believe in nonviolently.

While watching the movie I gained a lot of insight about what it's like to be mistreated and underprivileged, but I had never really thought about the strength and power it took to overcome these tribulations. Every day of my life I experience other people's mistreatment and even sometimes my own, and it is the worst feeling in the world to not be able to change it and feel overpowered. However, I no longer complain. I have learned now that action does speak louder than words, so instead I gather my thoughts and spread knowledge among those that are intimidated by authority. The African Americans in Nashville fought for their freedom and American status. They encouraged me to believe that all things are worth fighting for, even the small things. In further thought, the nonsense that goes on at my job allows me to step one foot in the door. For example, a majority of my co-workers feel threatened by the management staff, who abuse their authority to the max. Therefore, I took it upon myself to write a letter to the district manager of the company. But it does not stop there; I am now held accountable to speak on behalf of the staff at the next store meeting.

In conclusion, I now know that the struggle may be long and may unfortunately have no result, but it is worth the defeat. Nobody in this world should have to live their life without dignity, but sadly to say, it happens. More people should realize that life is worth fighting for no matter what the circumstances. However, what we must remember is that you kill evil with kindness, nonviolently. Nothing in this world will ever be equal, but with inspiring people like Gandhi and Diane Nash, the power, strength, and courage is all mine.

- L. O.

Respect

I hold the utmost degree of respect for the Fisk University students, their supporters concerning the events in Nashville, as well as for Gandhi, his supporters, and their persistent efforts to bring about change through nonviolence. This is truly remarkable, because I feel so few are capable of achieving change by this method. That is, pursuing change in defiance of the status quo and the oppression that accompanies it. It takes quite a unique individual, and furthermore an individual who is part of something much larger, who is one soul joined with the souls of many others in unison to further the movement.

When most people think of nonviolence movements the name Martin Luther King Jr. virtually always comes to mind first, and the 1960s peace marches and sit-ins join those first thoughts. For most, Gandhi's movements are overshadowed by those of the 1960s, yet essentially it all began with Gandhi 30 years earlier and one could say that his policies served as a model for those who were soon to begin in our country. I admire him because he was the first to demonstrate that sacrifices would have to be made for the ultimate betterment of the majority.

In the (psychology) textbook this is defined as altruism. I do not observe too many practicing this today. The decrease of morally sound individuals and the increase of greedy individuals are in part what our society has come to today. Some may argue that perhaps we see less altruism today because there is less in terms of legal injustices to protest, but I disagree. I feel there is much to be done and I remember it every time I drive down the street and see a police vehicle. Unfortunately, I do not feel that we will ever approach this kind of greatness again. The world is much more violent than it has ever been, and that is reflected in people's refusal to cooperate with one another and in their actions towards one another.

For the type of movement we saw in Nashville in 1960 and for the greater part of the decade was systematic. There was concern that if one or two people lost their nerve and submitted to violence, it would have jeopardized the whole thing. It was mentioned in the documentary that this is what their opposition wanted to see happen. They saw it as a passing fad, and thought it would soon go away with arrests, beatings, and other forms of intimidation. Instead it has gone down in history as something much more, because of the exercise of moral discipline and teamwork.

- M. M.

Taught Me A Lot

In the PBS special we watched two segments both dealing with nonviolent protest. The first segment dealt with segregation in Tennessee and the second segment was about Gandhi. Both segments taught me a lot about nonviolence.

In the first episode, we watched the segregation in Tennessee. The episode taught all about nonviolent demonstration. The demonstrators used different means other than violence to get their message across to the white members of the community. The black demonstrators first tried to desegregate counters in restaurants. The way they did this was by using three groups of people that came in, one group after the other groups were arrested. The second episode was about Gandhi and how he marched members of his movement to the sea. While watching Gandhi I did not really agree with him, because all he did was march and collect different members throughout the communities. I did agree with how he asked different members of the government to step down from their positions. I did agree with this because it breaks down the chain of command.

Before I watched this movie the only kind of demonstrations I was used to was the violent type. I have watched on television the L.A. riots as well as many other ones. I never realized that it could be done in a nonviolent way. By watching these segments it showed me that more is accomplished from nonviolence than violence. Not as many people die, and people get their message across more effectively by not hurting anyone. This really shows me that they stand for what they believe in.

- J. H.

What is "Normal"?

While watching these videos in class, I can feel myself wishing it were more like this everywhere. It can be hard for some to relate to this nonviolent method of bringing changes to the world. I would guess this goes back as far as when we were children. The *Tough Guise* issue would also apply here.[12] If we were not taught to fight with weapons and violence, if it were not "normal," how different things might be in the world. I once told my husband that if we were involved in a war, I would take my grandson far away so he would never have to kill another person or be killed himself. My husband was very upset by this and I really do understand why. He went into the Army right out of high school and made a career of it. He truly believes a man should fight for his country and protect his family. I too believe this, yet I pray for a different answer or a different method. People do what they feel to be normal or what they are taught to be right. He was raised to think this way like many men. How do we change this type of thinking?

In watching, I came to the conclusion that it took more bravery for those people to stand tough with no violence or weapons than it took for any of the officials with their clubs and guns at their sides. People who use force as a means to settle something are not using their God-given gift of thought. I realize these men are being given orders to use force, but this does not make it all right. Here is an example of Milgram's obedience study where we follow orders no matter who we hurt. We can also see Zimbardo's study is evident in how things can get carried away when a little power is involved.[13] Fear is also a big factor in how we react to a situation. We may be more forceful if we are more frightened.

People who use force and follow orders are only doing what is natural in this day and age. It is what we see all around us in every aspect of our life. If we started with our children in schools and showed them other ways to solve issues and ways of nonviolence, we may have a chance to change our current beliefs. Maybe if we showed both sides of an issue and how we have dealt with it in the past, children would see the nonviolent way as a better method. It is very hard to look at both sides of an issue when only one side is visible. I do not recall ever seeing one thing about nonviolent methods in all my years in school. This is the first time I have actually become aware of it. I had heard of Martin Luther King, Jr. And Gandhi but never really knew what they represented. Hopefully in our future years our children and their children will find a more peaceful way to communicate and discuss matters of the world.

- E. H.

Thoughts on the Reaction Papers

There are some themes in the students' writing that teachers of nonviolence will probably recognize. First, the students saw the relevance of nonviolence to core human concerns. There is eloquence in the way many of them expressed their feelings about these core concerns. There is an acknowledged lack of past education and information about nonviolence. There is amazement and disbelief that such important material would be withheld from children and from people generally. There are emotions such as anger evoked by the oppression against which nonviolence has often stood. There are insights derived, such as the idea that what seems

55

normal to us is determined by what we have been taught. There are corrections of belief, such as learning that not all "demonstrations" are violent. Important questions get raised, such as whether great leadership is necessary for nonviolence to be effective. Finally, there are fascinating individual variations in what people notice and emphasize, in how they feel, and in the conclusions they draw.

Nonviolence elicits strong feelings and significant, sometimes uncomfortable, thoughts about education and about life in general. It is a topic that stirs almost everyone to some degree, upon even brief exposure. Furthermore, most people find that they want to identify with the goals of nonviolence and to express their admiration for its struggles and accomplishments. It is remarkable that a subject not widely known or heard about can so quickly command sympathetic understanding, expressed in so many different ways.

Chapter 3 - What Goes On in a Nonviolence Training?

"Training" usually means a period of supervised practice in a skill or discipline, undertaken to achieve a higher degree of proficiency. We can see athletic, musical, vocational, and military training, among others, as fitting this definition of the term. Deliberately nonviolent thinking and acting are relatively unfamiliar, at least as skills, to most of us. Going through the experience of nonviolence training is an excellent way to become more familiar with nonviolence quickly.

Short-term nonviolence training has played an important role in preparing demonstrators and other workers in social change movements all over the world for what they would encounter as they set out to improve conditions in their communities. For some, whether they have been active in a social change movement or not, the initial experience of nonviolence training is also the beginning of a lifelong educational process leading to higher levels of mastery of this "third way" of thinking about life.[14]

"So, what do you actually do in one of these nonviolence trainings?" We get this question a lot. What follows is not a complete answer, because some of nonviolence training involves experiential and cooperative learning; that is, being right there in a training session or workshop with other people is much more powerful than reading about it. But there is no big mystery to nonviolence training, and here we will try to give a sense of how a workshop is put together and some of the content conveyed to the participants.

We will describe a workshop in Kingian Nonviolence, which is based on the work and writing of Martin Luther King, Jr. There are several other excellent approaches to nonviolence (for example, those of the American Friends Service Committee and the Fellowship of Reconciliation), and we regard the one described here as belonging to a family of related trainings. Some training approaches are Gandhian, some emphasize a religious tradition, some stress social change, and so on. Therefore, while the many varieties of nonviolence training and education do overlap, they are also complementary to each other. One approach will pay more attention to some aspects of nonviolence than others do, and together the different approaches make up a large mosaic of ideas and areas of application.

The Kingian approach described here was developed primarily by Dr. Bernard LaFayette, Jr., in collaboration with his colleagues David C. Jehnsen and Charles Alphin, Sr. Dr. LaFayette was an an active participant in the Civil Rights Movement, and worked closely with Dr. King.[15] In Dr.LaFayette's approach, an intensive two-day training experience is the preferred vehicle for introducing nonviolence while doing justice to King's ideas. Here is a typical sequence of topics for a two-day "core" workshop. This list will also serve as an outline of this chapter:

Topics in Kingian Nonviolence Training

Introduction of Participants
Finding Positive Common Ground
Analyzing Conflict: Types, Levels, and
Distances
Adversarial and Hegelian Understandings of
Conflict
Historical Perspective: Five Successful
Nonviolent Campaigns
King's Principles of Nonviolence
Steps for Nonviolent Problem-Solving
Using Top-Down and Bottom-Up Planning
Large-Scale Group Exercise
Closing

Trainers are often asked to present shorter workshops, and the content would then be abbreviated. However, even in a shortened training or presentation we would include some historical perspective on Martin Luther King's work, the Principles of Nonviolence, and the Steps for Nonviolent Problem Solving.

Using the full list of topics, let us go through the two-day training plan, and consider each component in turn.

Introduction of Participants

The initial introduction of group members to one another is treated, not as preliminary to the training, but as one of its integral stages. Introductions are done in such a way that individuals begin to learn about each other as people, get on their feet and talk, and get a taste of standing in someone else's shoes. Our usual procedure is to have each group member talk with another person for about five minutes, and share answers to some specific questions such as "Where did you grow up?," "What is one thing that most people would never suspect about you?," and "Where would you go on your ideal vacation?" After this period of conversation, we ask each person to introduce their partner to the entire group, with a first-person twist: each person assumes the name and identity of their partner. So if Sally and Ron had been paired for the initial conversation, Sally would start her introduction by saying, "Hi, I'm Ron ... ," and then go on to relate what she has just learned about Ron, but in the first person.

After all the introductions have been made, the trainers can debrief by asking two kinds of questions. First are questions about what it was like to pretend to be someone else: Was this awkward? Why? Were you nervous about the correctness of the information you were giving? And so on. Second are questions about what it was like to be introduced by someone else: Did they "get" you? Were you appreciative that they listened to you so well? And so on. Each group of individuals will come up with its own insights about this exercise.

This type of introduction is a good ice-breaker both for groups of strangers and for groups of co-workers or students who are already acquainted with each other. Taking time for the conversations makes the process of getting started less rushed and more personal. Also, assuming the identity of another person gives a preview of "putting yourself in another's shoes," which is a meaningful skill for practicing nonviolence.

Finding Positive Common Ground

People have many positive qualities. They admire good qualities in others, such as strength, humor, quick-wittedness, compassion, and the ability to overcome adversity. They value their important relationships with friends and mentors, recognize the value of learning, and - across many religions and cultures - they understand that a reverence for life, the world, and others is a good thing. We often use an exercise early in the training workshop to establish that each person in the group has good values, that others do too, and that therefore there is reason to identify with other people and respect them and ourselves for being similar in good ways. There are several specific exercises that can help accomplish these goals. Our favorite is one we will call S/Heroes, a term meant to include both heroes (male) and sheroes (female).

We ask participants to think back over their own lives, and focus on people who have had a strong positive influence on them. To generate more s/heroes, we ask them to think of at least one important person from the first half of their life so far, and one from the second half. We also ask participants in the workshop to name the contribution each s/hero made to their lives, or the value the s/hero represents to them. Then we invite people to share who they have been thinking of, and why those s/heroes have been important to them.

One person might recall that his mother taught him how to make it through hard times. Another might say that her high school volleyball coach was the person who showed her that working hard produced results. Another might credit an older child at school as being the model for how to stay calm in a conflict. As each person contributes, we build lists of the s/heroes and values. Typically, as each person speaks, several others in the group will be seen nodding their heads in understanding. It is not unusual for a few tears to be shed as members of the group tell these mini-stories about their own lives.

Each person will speak from deep conviction, because these are stories from their own experience, and are key pieces of their own personal history. The nods and expressions of emotion from others in the group are an indication that this trading of stories touches something in each of us that could be called common ground - a "better side of human nature" that is not owned exclusively by some, but is almost universally shared by people everywhere.

Our better side needs to be supported, and one goal of nonviolence training is to provide that kind of support. Now, it is true that people have negative qualities too. Every day we receive many reminders that other people can mislead us or be dangerous to us. Our suspicions of others receive support from news stories about shootings and fights, road rage and domestic violence, corruption and brutality. Sometimes this negative bombardment makes it seem that there are two kinds of people, the good and the bad. But in fact, each of us contains both some of the good and some of the bad. In Martin Luther King's words, every one of us has the potential for both great good and great evil. The Russian novelist Alexander Solzhenitsyn expressed the idea this way:

"Gradually it was disclosed to me that the line

separating good and evil passes not through states, not between classes, nor between political parties either - but right through every human heart, and through all human hearts." [16]

We advise the members of our training group that the good side of an enemy, and therefore a large part of our potential commonality with him or her, is very easy to forget. The person that we dislike today almost certainly admires many of the same qualities that we do, and shares many positive qualities with us. But anger and hatred create a strong tendency to dehumanize our opponents. We forget that they are people like us. We also forget that they, or others like them, will still be there tomorrow, and we will again need to interact with them.

Remembering the humanity of our opponents, especially when we are angry, is another skill in the practice of nonviolence. Like other skills, it can be improved through practice. During training, we start the practice in a calm and friendly atmosphere. Most of us will benefit from further practice, however; the times when this skill is most needed are also the times when it will be most difficult.

Analyzing Conflict: Types, Levels, and Distances

Conflict is an inescapable part of life. Differences of perspective, experience, vested interest, ambition, and preference lead us to disagree with each other and to compete with each other. Sometimes human beings seem to crave conflict; we even invent new conflicts in the form of games, sports, and debates. Conflict can teach, invigorate, and entertain. However, we all know that conflict can also get out of hand. Arguments can escalate into violence. In order to understand the origins of violence, and our options for responding to it, it is helpful to take an analytical look at different types and levels of conflict, and at different distances from a conflict where a person may be located.

Types of Conflict

Let's look at four types of conflict, termed pathway, mutually exclusive, distributive, and value.

In a **pathway conflict**, the people who are in conflict actually have the same goal, but disagree over how to achieve it. For example, two friends may want to go to Cleveland to visit the Rock and Roll Hall of Fame. But one person wants to go as quickly as possible on the interstate highway, and the other wants to take a more scenic and leisurely route. Their conflict is not over where to go, but how to get there. **Mutually exclusive conflict** (also called goal conflict) involves people who disagree about their goals, but who must continue to function together because of family, work, or other ties. We ask our group to generate examples of pathway and goal conflicts in the family, at work, and in the community. **Distributive conflict** describes a situation in which there are not enough resources, and people are fighting for their share. A family example would be two teenagers both wanting to use their mother's car. **Value conflict** involves a fundamental disagreement over beliefs regarding right and wrong. The conflicts over abortion rights, gender equality, gun control, and capital punishment, are familiar examples.

Distinguishing different types of conflict can help us to discern what people still have in common (but are likely to forget or minimize), despite their current differences over paths, goals, resources, or values. For example, people in a pathway conflict have a common goal. People in a goal conflict are "stuck together" in the same family or workplace. People fighting over resources have their need for those resources in common. And people in a values conflict, as we have seen, share many positive human qualities that tend to be forgotten in the heat of battle.

It should be said that the types of conflict described here are not sharply and objectively different. To some extent viewing a conflict as one type rather than other is a choice. Most conflicts have a value dimension, especially to the participants. The important training outcome at this stage is acquiring the view that conflicts can be analyzed, and that the structure of the conflict may contain helpful clues for a participant, or an interested bystander, to move toward a solution.

Levels of Conflict

Second, it is useful to examine three levels of conflict that may affect a person's options for practicing nonviolence: normal, pervasive, and overt.

Normal conflict means disagreement or competition that is carried on within accepted rules. Participants want to win the conflict, but do not hate or despise their opponent. If people can be said to crave conflict, it must also be said that most of the time, it is normal conflict that they most desire – playing sports or games, debating with friends, and so on.

Pervasive or heated conflict occurs when tempers rise. The rules that govern normal conflict are tested and bent as emotions flood the participants' bodies, their voices get louder, their body language becomes combative or defensive, and their thoughts and words begin to dehumanize the opponent, setting that person up as a target to be attacked rather than a person deserving respect and consideration. **Overt** conflict involves actual fighting.

When does "violence" start? For many people, the third level, overt conflict, would be the very definition of violence. However, from the perspective of nonviolence, it is at the second level, pervasive or emotionally heated conflict, that violence emerges and the need to control it begins. Kingian Nonviolence does not define normal conflict as a form of violence. Thus, it is possible, and even desirable, to have normal pathway, goal, distributive, and value conflicts - all without violence.

The goal of nonviolence is not to eliminate conflict. In fact, sometimes the goal is to create it. As practitioners of nonviolence, we are interested in maintaining constructive effort at the normal level of conflict, preventing escalation to the other levels, and intervening to de-escalate to the normal level when necessary. In order to do this, we must develop skills for managing conflict.

In a workshop, we may point toward this need for learning skills using role-playing exercises on identifying types and levels of conflict. One or two pairs of participants act out a conflict, and others observe and try to classify the type and level that is being portrayed. Based on this analysis, we then discuss approaches for managing or solving the conflict.

Distance from a Conflict

A third dimension of conflict is a person's distance from it. You may be in the very middle of it as a **participant**, or nearby watching it unfold as a **bystander**, or you may be farther away as a **remote observer**. For each of these distances, there would be a range of nonviolent options. Importantly, this range of options widens as distance from the conflict increases. This means that a participant in conflict may have very few options, a bystander more options, and a remote observer many. Now, although the remote observer has the most opportunity to change the conditions and even the social structures that lead to conflict, he or she may also have little motivation to do so. Motivation, meaning the urgency with which a person seeks to solve the conflict, diminishes with distance, being greatest for participants, less for bystanders, and least for remote observers.

Let us briefly consider the options available to bystanders, who are often in the best position to intervene in conflicts constructively. William Ury, an authority on negotiation, has listed ten roles that a "third side" can play in a conflict. Three of these roles pertain to prevention, and so are relevant early in the development of a conflict: the provider, the teacher, and the bridge-builder. Four of the roles pertain to resolving ongoing conflict: the mediator, the arbiter, the equalizer, and the healer. Finally, three of the roles address the containment of conflict: the witness, the referee, and the peacekeeper. For more on these roles, we recommend Ury's book, *Getting to Peace*.[17]

Adversarial and Hegelian Understandings of Conflict

Most of us perceive conflict in terms of two adversaries opposed to each other. That is, we assume that the conflict is a contest between these two sides, and that one side will win and the other lose. Martin Luther King was influenced by the philosopher G.W.F. Hegel to view conflict in another way. Consider this quote from one of Dr. King's sermons:

"But life at its best is a creative synthesis of opposites in fruitful harmony. The philosopher Hegel said that truth is found neither in the thesis nor the antithesis, but in an emergent synthesis which reconciles the two." [18]

The terms thesis, antithesis, and synthesis are from Hegel's treatment of how conflicts evolve over time. The perspective offered by Hegel is that conflicts have a past and a future; the contest we see before us in the present is part of a larger whole. Today's contest between two adversaries is like a still picture taken out of a movie. Unlike artificial conflicts such as a baseball game, the two sides in a real everyday conflict may both win, or they may both lose. They may not even stay the same people throughout the conflict, because of changes in their knowledge or interests. Conditions may also change because of the intervention of other people. When a new synthesis, a third position acceptable to both of the adversaries, is found, both sides win.

Dr. King saw opportunity in this way of viewing conflict. He suggested that creative, nonviolent leadership could often shape the progress of conflicts toward reconciliation of the original adversaries.

How can we discover a synthesis that can reconcile the conflicting positions of thesis and antithesis? There is no formula that will guarantee a satisfactory result. However, there is an approach that is worth trying, and we introduce it in training as a way of turning the Hegelian view of conflict into a rational procedure. In this approach, we look for "threads of truth" - that is, valid points or legitimate needs and interests - in both thesis and antithesis. Combining the threads of truth from the two opposed positions can give us a "first draft" of a synthesis. At the very least, this exercise gives a third way to look at the overall problem.

Dr. King used this approach to derive an understanding of nonviolence itself. Many times, people are faced with a threat or offense, and feel they must decide between fighting back or just letting it go without responding; they experience an internal conflict, in which the thesis is violence, and the antithesis is passivity. Now, what is a truth, or a good quality, about violence? Well, violence is at least active; it involves doing something in response to an injustice. What is a truth, or a good quality, about passivity? Well, passivity is unlikely to hurt people through direct retaliation against the aggressor or the collateral damage that would follow it. Nonviolence, in Dr. King's derivation, combines the activity of violence with the non-injury of passivity; it is an active response to injustice that seeks no harm. In this way, Dr. King was able to explain nonviolence to his followers, and to clear up for them the mistaken notion that nonviolence means passively letting injustice happen. Furthermore, from their knowledge of Dr. King's accomplishments, his listeners could see that most of those achievements fit this definition.

Historical Perspective

The most active period of the Civil Rights Movement was 1955-1968, the years during which Dr. King and others led campaigns to end legal segregation of the races in the southern United States. A nonviolence workshop cannot teach all of this history, but we do sketch the stories of five campaigns that illustrate the successful use of nonviolence training in community change: the Montgomery bus boycott, the Nashville sit-ins, the Freedom Rides, the Birmingham civil rights campaign, and the Selma voting rights campaign. For each campaign, we aim to review the issue that was addressed, identify some of the people involved, describe the methods used, and be clear about the result that was achieved. We encourage our participants to study the history of nonviolence in greater detail; for many, this becomes an enduring avocation.

Montgomery, 1955-56

In Montgomery, Alabama in 1955, the city bus system was segregated under local law, and was notorious in the city's black community for daily mistreatment and humiliation of non-white riders. On December 1, 1955, Rosa Parks was arrested for refusing to give up her seat on a city bus to a white person. Martin Luther King, Jr., a recently-arrived pastor, was chosen to head the Montgomery Improvement Association, which organized a boycott of the city buses that lasted for 381 days. The boycott was opposed by leaders of the white community, and by white supremacists who bombed Dr. King's home. Dr. King insisted on nonviolence throughout the boycott, and won national attention and support for the cause of desegregation. A Supreme Court decision late in 1956 declared the segregated bus system unconstitutional, ending the boycott.

Nashville, 1960

The famous tactic of "sitting in" at segregated lunch counters did not start first in Nashville; sit-ins had been used sporadically at least since the 1930s as an attempt to change race-based discrimination. However, in February 1960 the famous Greensboro NC sit-ins at Woolworths set off a wave of sit-ins across the United States. Nashville's sit-ins were led by a remarkable group of young college and seminary students, including Diane Nash, John Lewis, and Bernard LaFayette Jr., who had been studying nonviolence under Jim Lawson, and preparing for a challenge to segregation in their city. Peaceful sit-ins at several downtown lunch counters were followed by a general boycott that drastically affected business during the pre-Easter shopping season. After the racially motivated bombing of the home of Z. Alexander Looby, the students' legal counsel, there was a march of several thousand protesters to City Hall, where Diane Nash confronted the mayor, Ben West, and asked him directly whether he could personally defend segregation. He declared that he could not, and from that point on, the desegregation of central Nashville made progress. The students from the Nashville group went on to play major roles in other campaigns of the Civil Rights Movement - some, including Bernard LaFayette, serving on Dr. King's staff.

Freedom Rides, 1961

The Freedom Rides were undertaken in 1961 to challenge southern states to enforce federal laws desegregating interstate bus facilities such as washrooms and waiting rooms in bus stations. James Farmer, head of the Congress of Racial Equality (CORE), decided to draw attention to the still-segregated facilities by having a mixed group of black and white people ride Greyhound and Trailways buses from Washington DC to New Orleans. The Freedom Riders were violently attacked in Alabama at Anniston, again in Birmingham, and again in Montgomery. Trained in nonviolence, they did not retaliate in kind. Additional riders, beginning with trained student leaders from Nashville, joined the Rides. They were determined that violence would not succccd against the effort to desegregate interstate transportation. As a result of the Freedom Rides, Attorney General Robert Kennedy instructed the Interstate Commerce Commission to actually enforce the law, and desegregate the busing facilities. Signs for separate "Whites Only" and "Colored" facilities began to disappear.

Birmingham, 1963

In 1963, one hundred years after President Lincoln's Emancipation Proclamation officially ended most slavery, Birmingham, Alabama was, according to Dr. King, the most segregated city in America. The downtown business district allowed black citizens to spend money, but not to sit at lunch counters or to use the stores' fitting rooms or washrooms. Martin Luther King Jr., Fred Shuttlesworth, and others led a boycott of the downtown businesses seeking to desegregate stores and increase their hiring of black employees. There were marches and demonstrations, resulting in the arrests of many people, including Dr. King. It was during this campaign that he wrote the famous Letter From Birmingham Jail. Marches across Kelly Ingram Park by young demonstrators were met by police violence in the form of dogs and fire hoses ordered by the commissioner of public safety, Eugene "Bull" Connor. This greatly embarrassed President Kennedy's administration in its international efforts to promote American values. An agreement was eventually negotiated between Dr. King and the city, which served as a preview of the federal Civil Rights Act of 1964.

Selma, 1965

The voting rights of black people in the south were severely restricted, and this further diminished their ability to serve on juries and run for public office. Thus, gaining and exercising the right to vote constituted a critical step in the push for greater racial justice. The campaign in Selma, Alabama in 1965 was part of a major effort by the Southern Christian Leadership Conference, the Student Nonviolent Coordinating Committee, and other groups, to increase the number of black citizens who were registered to vote. Martin Luther King, John Lewis, Hosea Williams, Ralph Abernathy, and other leaders organized three attempts to march from Selma to Montgomery, the state capitol. On Bloody Sunday, March 7, the marchers were beaten by police and a mounted posse as they crossed the Edmund Pettus Bridge. Television broadcasts showing nonviolent demonstrators being ridden down and beaten shocked millions of viewers. The final march to Montgomery took place two weeks later with participants from across the nation, including many clergy (author Ira Zepp was one) who returned home and preached about voting rights and citizenship. The Selma campaign led directly to passage of the federal Voting Rights Act of 1965, which made barriers to voter registration and voting illegal.

A Note on Martyrs of the Movement

Three people died during the Selma campaign. The first was Jimmy Lee Jackson, 26, a deacon in his Baptist church, who was shot by a police officer after a peaceful demonstration in Marion, Alabama during the early days of the campaign. The second was Rev. James Reeb, 38, who was attacked by segregationists the evening following Dr. King's second march to the Edmund Pettus Bridge, which had ended with prayer and a return to Selma in observance of a court injunction. The third was Viola Liuzzo, 39, a housewife and civil rights activist from Detroit who had come to Selma as a volunteer to help with the voting rights campaign by serving as a driver. After the completion of the third march, she was shot and killed by the Ku Klux Klan while driving with another civil rights worker, Leroy Moton. Moton survived by pretending to be dead.

Rev. Reeb and Viola Liuzzo were both members of the Unitarian Universalist denomination. Ever since the Selma campaign, the UU church has taken a special interest in civil rights history, and especially the cause of voting rights for which Jimmy Lee Jackson, James Reeb, and Viola Liuzzo gave their lives.

Challenging a society that is willing to violently resist you in your work for justice can obviously be frightening. These deaths reinforce the fears of many people that standing up for a cause nonviolently is a dangerous thing to do - and indeed it is.

However, during the 14-year period from 1954 to 1968, relatively few people died in the U.S. struggle for civil rights, at least when compared to the much larger number of deaths in leaderless riots at home or in the wars of that time abroad. Just forty names appear on sculptor Maya Lin's Civil Rights Memorial at the Southern Poverty Law Center in Montgomery, Alabama. A book published by the Center tells the stories of these 40 martyrs.[19]

Principles of Nonviolence

The heart of this Kingian nonviolence training can be found in the chapter called "Pilgrimage to Nonviolence," in Martin Luther King's first book, <u>Stride Toward Freedom</u>.[20] Dr. King pauses in the middle of his book about the Montgomery bus boycott to explain the development of his approach to nonviolence. He reviews his educational history and some of the intellectual influences he carried away from his studies at Morehouse College, Crozer Theological Seminary, and Boston University.[21] Dr. King positions himself in critical opposition to both capitalism and communism, although he finds valuable ideals in both. He distinguishes nonviolence from pacifism. And then, in the last few pages of the chapter, he presents six principles of nonviolence that, for him, are the guiding principles of the boycott and of his overall mission. In nonviolence training we present these principles, and get our groups to alternately challenge and defend them.

Martin Luther King's Six Principles of Nonviolence

King's Principles speak both to the nature of nonviolence and to some of our most deeply rooted fears.

They also address some serious misunderstandings that many people have about how their lives intersect with those of others. Here is the list of principles; alternative wordings, including Dr. King's own phrases, are given that express the main ideas for different audiences.

1. **Nonviolence is a way of life for courageous people.** In Dr. King's words, "… nonviolence is not a method for cowards." For young people: Nonviolence takes courage.

2. **The Beloved Community is the framework for the future.** In Dr. King's words, "… (nonviolence) does not seek to defeat or humiliate the opponent, but to win his friendship and understanding." For young people: Turn enemies into friends.

3. **Attack the forces of evil, but not the people who are doing evil.** In Dr. King's words: "… the attack is directed against the forces of evil rather than against persons …" For young people: Focus on the problem, not on "problem people."

4. **Accept suffering without retaliation for the sake of the cause.** In Dr. King's words: "… a willingness to accept suffering without retaliation, to accept blows from the opponent without striking back." For young people: Every good thing has a cost. For police and military trainees: Sacrifice may be necessary.

5. **Avoid internal violence of the spirit as well as external physical violence.** In Dr. King's words: "… (nonviolence) avoids not only external physical violence but

also internal violence of the spirit. … At the center of nonviolence stands the principle of love." For young people: Cultivate love to replace hatred.

6. **The universe is on the side of justice.** In Dr. King's words: "… (nonviolence) is based on the conviction that the universe is on the side of justice. Consequently, the believer in nonviolence has deep faith in the future." For young people, and for volunteers who risk burnout: Justice is possible, so keep at it.

Sample Objections to Each of King's Principles

King's six principles challenge human beings to take a moral "high road." While they are obviously nice ideas, and social pressure may lead some to pay lip service to them, the principles are not taken seriously by many people under normal circumstances – at least, not at first. Occasionally, through hard experience or through sudden insight, people are won over on their own to the view of life that the principles exemplify.

Waiting for sudden insight is not a recommended teaching strategy, however. Another path is to spend some time during nonviolence training on both the reasons for adopting these ideals and the practical difficulties of living up to them. Interestingly, upon hearing the principles, most people inwardly recognize that they want to accept them, but fear that the real world makes it too difficult to do so. Here are some typical "but" reactions to each principle:

1. **Nonviolence Takes Courage**

But: "Nonviolence means not wanting to fight. Sounds like being a coward to me."

2. **The Beloved Community**

But: "Community? Why should I put up with people I don't like?"

3. **Attacking Evil, not People**.

But: "What about evil people? Don't they deserve to be attacked?"

4. **Suffering may be Necessary**.

But: "Isn't it stupid to let yourself - a good person - get hurt?"

5. **Internal Violence and Love**.

But: "My feelings are what they are, violent or not. It's healthy to let them out."

6. **A Just Universe**.

But: "Are you kidding? The world is going to hell in a handbasket."

These common objections reveal some strong initial resistance to nonviolence. Note that several of the objections reveal feelings of distrust and fear. Remarkably, we often defend ourselves against nonviolence as if it were a threat to us! One of the reasons Martin Luther King stood out as a great leader is that he challenged this resistance. He suggested that the reasons for nonviolence are so strong that we need to overcome our fears of it. How would Dr. King answer the objections listed above, and others like them?

That question can be turned into a training exercise. Let us consider each objection in turn, and how Dr. King, or someone thinking very much like him, would respond to it.

Imagining Dr. King Responding to Each Objection

In a training workshop, participants would spend time in small groups generating challenging questions about King's Principles, similar to those we have just imagined. Then, working on the questions posed by others, each group would try to formulate some answers to the questions, answers that Dr. King himself might have given. This practice in "thinking like King" avoids pressuring people into a premature uncritical acceptance of nonviolence, and provides insight into nonviolence as a way of thinking that can be learned.

To illustrate some possible products of this exercise, here are some responses to the objections that were given to each principle, written while imagining how Martin Luther King's voice might have sounded in expressing a nonviolent perspective.

Objection to Principle 1, which is about courage: **Nonviolence means not wanting to fight. Sounds like being a coward to me**.

Response: *Courage is often tied up in the desire to be a man, and so the first principle is primarily directed to those who have this desire. But young boys, full of bravado and physical courage, are*

79

often frightened by the prospect of embarrassment and ridicule. Once a mean-spirited bullying mood sets in among their friends, they are compelled by this fear to go along. Is this courage? No. It is conformity to peer pressure.

(Now, it must be said that peer pressure is just as strong for most adults as it is for these young boys. But we often talk unfairly about the young as if peer pressure were exclusively their problem.)

The courage referred to in the first principle is often not physical courage, but the courage to act rightly rather than in conformity with group pressure.

On the other hand, the readiness to fight is often not a sign of courage, but a giving-in to impulse, panic, and expectations.

Nonviolence asks us to measure our responses to others, and not to be confused about what requires courage.

Objection to Principle 2, which is about the "beloved community": **Community? Why should I put up with people I don't like?**

Response: *The second principle provides a test that we can all use to determine whether we are moving toward this ideal called the beloved community, or away from it. The test is this: Are we seeking to defeat and humiliate our opponent? Or are we trying to win his friendship and understanding? If the first answer is "No," and the second answer is "Yes," then we are heading in the right direction.*

That is, how we act toward our enemies is the test of whether we are moving toward or away from the world envisioned by nonviolence.

It is admittedly difficult to look beyond the moment and decide to treat our enemy decently. But that is precisely what nonviolence challenges us to do.

In the thoughtful words of Abraham Lincoln, "Am I not destroying my enemies when I make friends of them?"

Objection to Principle 3, which is about attacking problems, not people: **What about evil people? Don't they deserve to be attacked?**

Response: *The third principle asks us to keep "personalities" out of our efforts to solve problems. Here we must remember that people are not simply good or bad, but a complex mixture of traits and tendencies. Although human beings have a tendency to demonize their enemies, this tendency does little to resolve conflicts, and often escalates them unnecessarily.*

We are often diverted from solving problems because we fix our emotional energy on revenge against individuals, and because upon getting our revenge by hurting or incarcerating the guilty, we just stop.

Studies of violent criminals support the idea that even very "bad" men are a tragic mixture of beliefs, defenses, and vulnerabilities which invite sympathy upon close examination, and which hold clues to rehabilitation.[22] The terrible damage done by some of these inmates is evidence not just of personal depravity but of external conditions that, if changed, could have averted the damage. Their stories are instructive about how we could prevent violence by changing the conditions out of which it grows.

Why should we stop attacking persons, when that feels like such a natural thing to do? We should stop because that kind of attack sets up a continuing cycle of hostile retaliation, and does nothing to bring greater justice or to solve the problems in which both we and our opponents are enmeshed.[23]

Objection to Principle 4, which is about suffering: **Isn't it stupid to let yourself - a good person - get hurt?**

Response: *We must acknowledge that many people seem to experience a great fear of nonviolence, because they suspect that a commitment to nonviolence may call for suffering. This suffering may occur when a nonviolent person is attacked by a violent person. More commonly, it may occur whenever a nonviolent person stands up and puts him- or herself in an uncomfortable position for a good cause.*

However, it should be emphasized that the fourth principle does not send people out to endure suffering for its own sake. There is already plenty of suffering in the world, some of it accidental and some of it intentional. Most of this suffering, especially the intentional kind, is unnecessary.

The suffering at issue is the purposeful suffering, or sacrifice, that may be necessary to right a wrong, and which therefore can be redemptive, not only for the person who suffers, but for others as well.

In our real world, the choice to be nonviolent may lead to suffering for the sake of a just cause. But the choice to be violent always leads to suffering, usually to no good purpose.

Objection to Principle 5, which is about replacing violent feelings with love: **My feelings are what they are, violent or not. It's healthy to let them out.**

Response: *It is true that human beings are susceptible to* *strong feelings of resentment and hostility. Many people believe reflexively that these feelings constitute a force of nature that cannot, and even should not, be controlled.*

But we are not entirely helpless in the face of these emotions. We have the power to cultivate the kind of love called agape as a benevolent emotion to replace internal violence of the spirit. And we have the obligation to do so.

People steer their own emotional lives all the time. We do this by spending time with our family and friends, through meditation and prayer, and with music and reading and reflection.

The violence that we seek to replace with nonviolence originates within the human heart. Our resentments and hatred therefore hurt us first, and most. Fortunately, we have the ability to steer away from this violence within us, by reminding ourselves of the humanity of our enemies, and by engaging in the important work of enlisting their help in the cause of justice.

Objection to Principle 6, which is about progress toward justice: **Are you kidding? The world is going to hell in a handbasket.**

Response: *For many of us, there is a religious foundation for the belief that the universe is on the side of justice. Therefore, it is perhaps easier for the faithful to be confident about this principle than it is for more secular proponents of nonviolence.*

One secular way to think about this principle is in terms of what world people would prefer to live in. Imagine that the events in the human universe can be sorted into five boxes: the intentionally good, the accidentally good, the neutral, the accidentally bad, and the intentionally bad. When asked to change the universe by throwing out one box, almost everyone chooses to discard the box containing intentionally bad events. This strong preference is evidence that the scales of the universe are tipped toward the good.

Now, the universe may lean toward justice, but that is not enough. The universe is full of tools, but they will be ineffective unless we pick them up and use them. We must pick them up, use them, and keep on using them. And that brings up the value of persistence.

This sixth principle is important because persistence in the face of resistance is important. Frustration, at least for a while, is the inevitable consequence of challenging the status quo. And the duration of this frustration is uncertain. Combating burnout among those who work for justice and human betterment is a constant mental health issue, which leaders of a movement must acknowledge and confront.

But here is the good news. Persistence works. The great examples of social change of the past hundred years or more have happened at tipping points in our history, prepared for by years of quiet work beforehand. We may not be able to predict when these points will come, but we can be confident that working steadily for justice will one day bring the needed change.

Aggression and Conciliation

The Aggression-Conciliation Model is an outgrowth of Dr. King's second and third principles. The second principle is about treating your opponent in a conflict as a potential ally. The third principle is about not personally attacking human beings whose actions may have been evil, but instead attacking the evil in unjust situations.

The Model looks like this:

YOU		PROBLEM
Aggression	==>	Conditions
Conciliation	==>	Persons

Let's say that YOU (on the left side of the diagram) face a PROBLEM (on the right). Broadly speaking, you have two large sets of possible responses to the problem. The first, Aggression, consists of all the high-energy, attacking, oppositional things that you are capable of. The second, Conciliation, consists of all the ways you can be accepting and respectful.

The Problem also has two parts, called Conditions and Persons. Conditions are what some scholars call the "systemic" or "structural" aspects of the Problem, which exist regardless of the people who are involved. Persons are the individuals who play roles that enforce or benefit from those conditions, the actors that you confront at the present moment.

The diagram of the Aggression-Conciliation Model shows a guide for how to direct your responses appropriately with the aim of solving the Problem. Two conscious choices are recommended: directing your Aggression toward the Conditions (which echoes King's third principle), and directing your Conciliation toward Persons (which echoes King's second principle).

The model also recommends that two errors be avoided: directing Aggression toward Persons, which tends to set up a cycle of hostility and violence, and directing Conciliation toward Conditions, which amounts to accepting the Problem without trying to solve it.

Participants in a workshop can be asked to analyze a community or family conflict and make recommendations for how it might be handled differently, using the Aggression-Conciliation Model as a guide. Some examples: People in a poor neighborhood might resent the owner of a convenience store, the only place within walking distance where they can buy food. Or: A mother has daily fights with her daughter over the loud music she plays after school. Or: Freshman college roommates are in conflict over how to control the traffic of friends who visit their dorm room.

The Aggression-Conciliation Model is appealing because of its symmetry and completeness in comparison to other approaches. We have found that the Model can help to dispel the misconception that nonviolence wants people to completely suppress their anger and aggression. For example, a young man approached one of us after a workshop and thanked the trainers especially for teaching him about aggression and conciliation. He explained that the model did more than just repeat the often-heard demand that he not fight with people. The part about directing Aggression toward Conditions, he said, "gives me something to do with my anger."

Finally, it is important to keep in mind that the Persons on the right side of the diagram also have a choice to make about how to use their own capacities for Aggression and

Conciliation. In fact, to them, you are really one of the Persons who is part of their "Problem." Both of you possess human strengths and weaknesses that it behooves you both to understand. One is that a Hegelian view of conflict offers more options than an adversarial view. Another is that behavior tends to be reciprocated, so that choosing Aggression or Conciliation increases the likelihood that your opponent will choose likewise. Another is that persistence increases your chances of successfully solving the problem, as suggested by Dr. King's sixth principle.

Now, the Aggression-Conciliation Model is not guaranteed to solve your problems quickly; it is only a framework within which some elements of nonviolent problem solving can be assembled and put to work.

Steps for Nonviolent Problem-Solving

Martin Luther King Jr.'S famous *Letter from Birmingham Jail* is a classic essay on purposeful action. It was written as a response to members of the white clergy who had urged Dr. King and his colleagues to avoid confrontation, and instead wait for the gradual progress of civil rights in Birmingham. Dr. King replied in his *Letter* that the time had come for action, and explained that the actions of the campaign to desegregate Birmingham were not impulsive, but the result of a deliberate planning process.

He listed the four steps of this process as follows: "… collection of the facts to determine whether injustices exist; negotiation; self-purification; and direct action." [24] In the training curriculum used today, nonviolent problem-solving is discussed using a framework of six steps whose roots lie in Dr. King's <u>Letter</u>.

Six Steps for Nonviolent Problem-Solving:

- **Information Gathering**, also known as Research

- **Education**, involving both Teaching and Learning

- **Personal Commitment**, requiring Reflection and Resolve

- **Negotiation**, to arrive at a Common Description of the Problem

- **Direct Action**, if necessary, to Restart Negotiations

- **Reconciliation**, in which people establish a better Relationship

These steps are meant to be applicable from the individual and family levels to the community and global levels. They stand in contrast to impulsive, hostile, threat-driven responses to problems. The steps are consistent with many prescriptions for rational problem-solving found in business, psychology, and philosophy.

Information Gathering

The first step in nonviolent problem solving - Information Gathering – derives from Dr. King's phrase "collection of the facts." Often problems can be solved through Information Gathering alone. However, this step deserves some discussion.

From the calm perspective of a reader at home, or a student sitting in a classroom, it may seem obvious that a person should gather information when presented with a problem or a conflict. But information gathering is seldom what people actually do when confronted with an angry neighbor who has a grievance, or a car that won't start, or being fired from a job, or being threatened by harassing phone calls. Our first reaction to being faced with an emotionally charged challenge is often some kind of emotional outburst rather than rational information seeking.

Our first impression of the problem — that is, the first idea we have about what we are facing - is often distorted. After all, we are under stress. Perhaps we have been surprised and knocked out of our familiar routine by the appearance of this new threat. The tendency to seek someone to blame kicks in. Our tendency to interpret conflicts as adversarial kicks in. Our physiology prepares us for fight or flight, and oversimplifies our thinking.

What advice might help a person to step back and start gathering information instead of reacting impulsively to the problem?

A short version of the advice we give is: "Doubt your first impression." The step of information gathering should start with a reminder of this simple suggestion. Training can build the habit of being skeptical about the truth of one's immediate perception of the situation at the beginning of almost any problem. That can open a path to more complete information gathering.

Why is this good advice?

Some of our thinking is fast - it is impressionistic and based on many ingrained assumptions and biases. Fast thinking can quickly reach decisions and guide action. Sometimes fast thinking saves our lives, but more often it leads us into trouble. There is another kind of thinking that is slower, more logical and investigative, and that gives up speed in order to achieve greater accuracy. Our first step of Information Gathering requires us to activate that second, slower, kind of thought. [25]

The need to actively seek out better information can be illustrated by examples generated by the training group. Ask, "Have you ever felt foolish because you jumped right into a conflict, making a totally wrong assumption about what was going on?" Most groups will have no trouble coming up with stories from their own experience, or second-hand stories from friends or from the news. These examples may reveal a variety of insights. Sometimes the information needed to solve a problem is "gathered" by accident, as when I discover the watch that I had thought stolen in the pocket of a pair of jeans I haven't worn for three weeks. Sometimes we change our impressions by learning about the perspective, needs, or motives of another person, as when the bus rider I had criticized for not giving up his seat to an elderly person finally gets up at his stop, retrieves his walker, and slowly leaves the bus using the handicap assist elevator. Sometimes the conflict is over data that is readily available but that no one has yet examined, as when a student challenges my long-held belief about the sources of pollution in the Great Lakes by locating an archive of excellent information on the subject that I had never consulted.

Another habit to develop is openness to different sources of information.

Gandhi famously held that in a conflict, each side owns a piece of the truth. That means we must be willing to accept a part of the solution from someone we regard as an opponent or even an enemy. On the scale of everyday arguments among friends or family members, a good way to put Gandhi's idea into action is to say "You have a point" when you've recognized a part of the truth in what they are saying. Said at the right moment, this simple statement has the power to defuse and re-channel the energy being invested in a conflict. It can also contribute to Information Gathering by you, and by the others in the situation.

Education

As information is being gathered, occasions will arise when the natural next step is to share that information with others. This is Education, an unstated but implicit part of Dr. King's "collection of the facts."

Every problem has stakeholders, people who are affected by the problem and have an interest (a stake) in solving it. The stakeholders are the audience. Information should be given to them that is verifiable, and that will help them contribute to the eventual solution.

It is important to be honest and open about Education. Education is not propaganda. It is not persuasion. It is not lying. Education should be the communication of good relevant information to those who need it, and who are in a position to use it.

At the same time, the message may need to be translated into the language of different groups of stakeholders, and framed to address their interests and ways of thinking. For example, the motivation for renovating a city's playgrounds may be most effectively strengthened among law enforcement officials by emphasizing public safety issues. But the approach to family service agencies might emphasize the benefits to children. The approach to city hall might emphasize the cost of various alternative plans. The same overall problem will look a little different to each of these stakeholder groups.

One is reminded of the fable of the elephant, in which different blind men each experienced the elephant in turn as a wall (because one felt the elephant's side), a tree (because one felt the elephant's leg), and a snake (because one felt the elephant's trunk). The perspectives of different observers will lead to different perceptions of the same reality.

The step of Education should be taken thoughtfully, and should include not only sending information out, but being open to suggestions from stakeholders that may come back in - a continuation of Information Gathering. In fact, these steps are never strictly sequential, but flow back and forth as the problem and its solution unfold.

It is interesting to reflect that Information Gathering is what scholars call "research," and Education is what most people would call "teaching." Research and teaching are the two principle missions of a college or university. When a college is at its best, research and teaching intertwine and inform each other. So should it be in a nonviolent problem solving process.

Personal Commitment

Personal Commitment is the step that Martin Luther King called "self-purification." Dr. King found through experience that difficult problems, once they were well understood, called for courage and strong personal commitment by the people attempting to solve them. For him, serious reflection and a conscious decision to go forward were absolutely necessary.

We have rarely found a step corresponding to Personal Commitment in textbooks on cognitive psychology, or in business school treatments of problem-solving. These disciplines implicitly take the personal commitment of the problem solver as a given. But in the real world, there are times when proceeding with an attempt to solve a problem will be premature and counterproductive. Deciding when and how to move, and whether you are the right person to do it, can determine the success or failure of the process. It is not difficult to see why Martin Luther King considered self-purification a necessary stage in the process of nonviolent problem-solving.

Sometimes the step of Personal Commitment will lead to a decision to go ahead, and sometimes the decision will be to postpone further steps if the problem is not "ripe" to be solved right now, or until additional people are available to join in the task, or other necessary conditions are in effect. In either case, it is important for the decision to be deliberate and based on a good understanding of the situation.

However, the deliberations of Personal Commitment should not be confused with procrastination. Dr. King's Letter from Birmingham Jail is a detailed reflection on the necessity to act. The Letter is a chapter in one of his books, whose very title is *Why We Can't Wait*.[26] The need to pause for a step of Personal Commitment is coupled with the need to be decisive.

A very important aspect of Personal Commitment is focusing on one tangible and specific goal at a time. During the Nashville sit-ins, there was a moment when Jim Lawson, giving his morning instructions to a group of demonstrators, told them to work in pairs, but to avoid pairing a white person "with a Negro of the opposite sex - because we don't want to fight that battle." At the time, interracial marriage was actually illegal in many states, and even the sight of an interracial couple could ignite opposition to the campaign over an issue not related to the desegregation of lunch counters.[27]

Regrettably, progressive causes often compete with each other for attention, money, time, and people. In a world with so many problems to solve, perhaps this is inevitable. However, in the pursuit of any one goal, it is important to keep the message simple and clear. Personal Commitment begins the process of taking one simple, well-considered step at a time toward a consciously chosen goal.

Negotiation

The step of Negotiation brings people with different positions together to discuss the problem, to offer proposals, and to more fully understand each other's underlying needs and interests. There are many treatments of negotiation as an art and a set of management skills. Most share the goal of moving the parties who are in conflict closer to a common description of the problem.

Negotiation involves difficult conversations, because the people involved disagree about important issues, and may have personalized the conflict so that they really don't like each other. They may fail to listen to what the other side is saying, and when both sides fall into this trap, little can be accomplished. One skill that helps is Active Listening, in which we consciously stop our own mental rehearsal of what we want to say next, and really listen to the person on the other side of the table. When it is our turn to speak, we first try to restate what we heard the other person saying, in a way that he or she will agree is their position. Only then will we respond to that position with ideas of our own. Active Listening can improve communication between the two sides by demonstrating respect, setting a standard for clarity, revealing competing and common interests, and creating movement toward solving real problems.

One popular approach to Negotiation that has a strong nonviolent flavor is described in the book *Getting to Yes*, by Roger Fisher and colleagues.[28] Like Martin Luther King, the authors of this book recommend close attention to one's opponent in a negotiation, seeking to understand the needs and interests that lie behind that person's public position. Also like Dr. King, *Getting to Yes* stresses the availability of win-win outcomes in most negotiating situations, and emphasizes the desirability of negotiating to a conclusion in which nobody walks away as a loser.

95

Direct Action

Sometimes, negotiations break down. Here is where the fifth step, Direct Action, may come in. The purpose of Direct Action is to return to the step of Negotiation. In Dr. King's words:

"You may well ask: 'Why direct action? Why sit-ins, marches, and so forth? Isn't negotiation a better path?' You are quite right in calling for negotiation. Indeed, this is the very purpose of direct action. Nonviolent direct action seeks to create such a crisis and foster such a tension that a community which has constantly refused to negotiate is forced to confront the issue."[29]

The "action" chosen should be appropriate to the problem at hand. Sometimes two nonviolent direct actions may take diametrically opposite forms. For example, in the Montgomery boycott people stayed off the city buses, but in the Freedom Rides people rode the interstate buses. Both were forms of Direct Action. In each case, the action was appropriate to the issue, and served to create tension toward changing entrenched segregation.

Note that Direct Action is not the centerpiece of nonviolence, although for many people examples such as sit-ins, boycotts, and marches are the first images that the word nonviolence may bring to mind. Direct Action is the fifth step, not the first. And it is only undertaken conditionally, if earlier steps have not solved the problem. Protests and demonstrations are sometimes carried out impulsively and out of strong emotional reactions to being offended or threatened. However, this type of direct action should be distinguished from actions that are in the spirit of nonviolence.

Some people will point to Dr. King's deliberate fostering of tension through direct action as evidence that he himself used pressure tactics to get what he wanted from his opponents. To these critics, creating tension and crisis does not seem to fit with their idea of nonviolence. In response to this position, we note that nonviolence is an active, not a passive, approach. We also note that in a democracy, using negotiation and nonviolent direct action stand in contrast to bullying by autocrats and bigots, which represents another approach to "problem-solving." Nonviolence achieves results through political rather than violent means, but without guaranteeing that the process will be comfortable for everyone.

Reconciliation

In Dr. King's *Letter From Birmingham Jail*, reconciliation was not mentioned as one of the preparatory steps he had taken before launching the 1963 desegregation campaign in that city. That makes sense, because reconciliation is about the outcome of nonviolent problem solving, not the "front end." At the time the *Letter* was written, Dr. King was still in the middle of the struggle.

Reconciliation represents a high standard for the outcome of a difficult struggle, especially one in which the parties have begun as enemies. To whatever extent possible, the solution of problems should move the parties closer to the Beloved Community – perhaps much closer, but perhaps only a little closer, for now. Full Reconciliation means that the original opponents in a conflict, and other stakeholders, can respect one another, understand each other's perspectives, and work together constructively.

A friend of ours who is a nonviolence trainer and a police lieutenant keeps the goal of Reconciliation in mind as he deals with perpetrators of crimes and with angry victims. He reports that the thought of Reconciliation tomorrow has a powerful effect on how he interacts with people today who would otherwise "push his buttons."

Often reconciliation is difficult to achieve in the short term. We may have to settle for a disgruntled compromise, or for people "agreeing to disagree," or for parties simply separating so that they do not continue to hurt each other, or for arbitration that leaves one side much less satisfied than the other. In many books, these outcomes count as conflict resolution. We prefer to think of them as temporary solutions that may eventually achieve nonviolent reconciliation. A helpful thought here is that problem-solving does not necessarily follow the timetable in my head, or yours.

Recall that Martin Luther King was influenced by the philosopher Hegel, and particularly by Hegel's dialectical way of viewing conflict. When we encounter a conflict, it appears to be a contest between two positions, the thesis and the antithesis. However, as time passes, these positions may evolve into a new position, the synthesis, which is different from either of the original two sides.

We can think of the step of Reconciliation as a kind of Hegelian synthesis. In the best case, it is a win-win solution to the original conflict, and may not only be a solution but a transformation of that conflict into a quite different situation.

Coordinating Top-Down and Bottom-Up Contributions

Many attempts to solve community problems fail because there is no knowledgeable and respected person on the scene with whom both community members and their political leaders can talk. Authority figures then are prone to make pronouncements that ring hollow to people living in neighborhoods. Average members of the community, who have important things to say, are disregarded by the leaders who have the power to implement their ideas. The people at the grassroots of the problem come to disrespect and caricature the officials in power, and the officials in turn disrespect and belittle the people they are supposed to serve. This kind of dysfunction is found in many communities all over the world.

From a nonviolence perspective, the built-in differences between official leaders and average community members create a continuing need for bringing "top" and "bottom" together. Nonviolent leadership can seek to bridge the gap between sides that are far apart by fostering more respectful communication. Some of the philosophy and skills of nonviolence introduced earlier in the training can now be applied to this type of situation.

It is very helpful to analyze the conflict using the vocabulary of nonviolence training. We ask our training group to remember that both leaders and ordinary community members are human beings with their own perceptions of the community and its problems. We remember that people may already be making the mistakes of personalizing the conflict (aggression toward persons) or apathetic withdrawal (conciliation toward conditions). We consider that both sides may have some valid points to make (threads of truth in both thesis and antithesis). We hold to the goal of getting people to work together (Principle 2 - seeking not to defeat and humiliate the opponent but to win his or her friendship and understanding). How can nonviolence guide two sides toward a good outcome (Step 6 - reconciliation)?

In general, the nonviolent leader or mediator uses the six steps and the aggression-conciliation approach with each side, repeatedly. With each side in turn, we demonstrate that we understand the problem from that side's point of view, including their needs and aspirations that may extend beyond the current problem. We seek to establish common ground from which the two sides can begin to work together on meeting shared needs.[30] We encourage each side to see the other as a potential ally rather than a permanent enemy. We also encourage each side to consider its relationship to such constituencies in the community as women and minority groups, youth and students, progressive and voluntary organizations, businesses, educational institutions, religious and interfaith settings, and government agencies.

This topic in the Kingian Nonviolence training program has traditionally been called "Top-Down, Bottom-Up." The image is of a nonviolent planner and mediator helping two sides with different roles in the community to create a synthesis out of their originally opposed positions. This role may or may not be successful on our timetable in any specific instance. But it is certain that many community problems have remained unresolved, and many misunderstandings between parts of a community have remained to fester for years, because the community lacked some members who were willing and able to play this role.

Large-Scale Exercise

Throughout a two-day training there are many opportunities for short role-playing exercises, in which group members can act out conflicts, or answer a question as if they were Martin Luther King, for example. Toward the end of the second day, we like to engage the group in a larger-scale exercise that can draw on several skills from the training. Here we describe two exercises, one, The Grid, that is suitable for a group of people that come from different life paths and work experiences, and one, Joy City, that is suitable for a group that already works together and faces real problems that they probably feel they know all too well.

The Grid

Legend has it that Albert Einstein invented a riddle that he thought only 1 or 2% of people would be able to solve. It belongs to a category called grid puzzles, and while they are very difficult for one person to solve alone, they can be somewhat more manageable, and instructive about group interactions, when several people are working on them.

Here is one grid puzzle, Einstein's famous "fish" riddle:

There is a row of five differently colored houses. Each house is occupied by a man with a different nationality. Each man has a different pet, prefers a different drink, and smokes a different brand of cigarettes. There are fifteen clues to aid in solving the riddle:

1. The Scot lives in the Red house.
2. The Swede keeps dogs as pets.
3. The Dane drinks tea.
4. The Green house is next to the White house, on the left.
5. The owner of the Green house drinks coffee.
6. The person who smokes Pall Mall cigarettes rears birds.
7. The owner of the Yellow house smokes Dunhill.
8. The man living in the center house drinks milk.
9. The Norwegian lives in the first house.
10. The man who smokes Blends cigarettes lives next to the one who keeps cats.
11. The man who keeps horses lives next to the man who smokes Dunhill.
12. The man who smokes Blue Master drinks beer.
13. The German smokes Prince.
14. The Norwegian lives next to the Blue house.
15. The man who smokes Blends has a neighbor who drinks water.

Who has fish at home?

Procedure: Print out the 15 clues and the question (i.e. "Who has fish at home?" - the answer to which is the goal of the exercise). Then cut the printed page into strips, each with one of the clues or the question on it. Distribute these slips to the members of the training group, going around repeatedly until all the strips have been given out. Members of the group are instructed not to show their slips to anyone else during the exercise. However, a whiteboard or other display board should be available for organizing information.

Then announce to the group that they have everything

they need. Don't answer any further questions.

A typical group will take anywhere from 30 to 60 minutes to solve a puzzle like this one. In the process, they will experience frustrations, and will recognize the need to negotiate over ways to represent the problem visually and incorporate pieces of information. It will be important for the group to ensure that everyone's input is included, because every single clue is needed to solve the puzzle. However, trainers should not give explicit coaching on such points.

Grid puzzles like this are logically solvable, but difficult enough to bring out complex human behavior. They require thoughtful information gathering and, depending on the group dynamics, may require all the other steps of nonviolent problem-solving in order to reach an answer that leaves everyone satisfied.

Joy City

The Joy City exercise can be adapted to the specific circumstances faced by the training group in their workplace or in the community outside the training. It will provide an opportunity for them to delve into familiar problems with the tools developed during the training. Here we sketch a Joy City exercise with hypothetical characteristics and problems to provide a sense of how this part of the training might play out. The details can be adapted to the needs of the actual training group.

Joy City is a medium-sized town of mixed cultures located about fifty miles from a much larger city in the same part of the U.S. where the group is meeting. There is one high school, grades 9-12, and one junior high school, grades 6-8. In the past few years the calls for police service, drug arrests, and homicides among youth have increased. There have been several fights at the high school since the school year started, and last evening, a young girl was killed by a stray bullet as she left the high school. Witnesses informed the police that a group of youths had been arguing in front of the school with guns just before the shooting started.

The training group is divided into small groups of 3 or 4 people each. The small groups are given 15-20 minutes to do the following:

(1) List information they would need to determine the causes of violence in Joy City.

(2) Indicate how they would involve community leadership and stakeholder groups.

(3) Decide how they would spend a one-time grant of $300,000 (or make actual use of some other significant but limited resource) toward solving the problems faced by the community.

The groups would be asked to work fast, without too much self-censorship, but to draw on the principles, the steps, and other components of the training as they work.

At the end of the small-group work, a trainer would call everyone together for a comparison of ideas. There will be plenty of opinions and a desire for discussion at this stage. Ideas will emerge that range widely in approach, emotional tone, and emphasis. Many proposals will indeed reflect the topics introduced during the training. It is unlikely that one approach will emerge that everyone agrees is the perfect solution. Almost everyone will feel that they have learned something valuable from ideas that others in the group have put forward.

An additional component of Joy City can be a period of Step 1 (information gathering) role playing, in which the small groups visit community officials such as the mayor and the police chief, to learn about their perspectives on the problem. Some individuals would be recruited to play the roles of these officials, and given tips on how to resist requests for information and action, based on such interests as keeping costs under control.

Toward the end of the exercise, most people in the group will be able to recognize ideas that illustrate the philosophy and methods of nonviolence. Where these ideas seem inadequate, group members will often point out how a proposal could be strengthened and still be nonviolent. The idea that **there may not be a perfect solution, but there are nonviolent approaches that are preferable to "enemy-thinking,"** can be voiced by a trainer, but the group will probably see this without the trainer's help.

Closing

At the end of our time with a training group, we like to form a circle and close the training in a way that allows people to reflect briefly on nonviolence and on their experience together. One way to do this is to ask each person to offer one word that captures their reaction to the training and their feelings about nonviolence. Some of the words that we often hear are energizing, humbling, inspiring, transforming, and worthwhile.

Of course, many group members are not able to summarize all their thoughts and feelings in one word. We have often instead heard lengthy dissertations. And that's OK, within reasonable limits.

Based on many training experiences, we have learned that an introduction to nonviolence along the lines we have described in this chapter has several positive effects on most of the members of a training group that they are aware of and appreciate:

- Participants are reminded through the values exercise that each person has good values, and that while there are differences between people, there is also positive common ground to be found.

- The historical perspective part of the training fills in gaps in almost everyone's knowledge of Martin Luther King Jr., about the legacy of the civil rights movement, and about the current concerns and functioning of communities, especially in the United States.

- Addressing conflict as more than just an adversarial head-butting contest, and linking Dr. King's view of conflict to the search for win-win solutions, is often a revelation.

- The training encourages people to examine their own beliefs and values, and to consider discrepancies between values and practices. It challenges people to consider their life choices and the strategies they choose for meeting their needs.

- The affirmation of personal worth and the acceptance of needs, combined with the challenge to change strategies, is almost always seen as an honest approach with real-world implications, that can appeal to at-risk youth and others who are resistant to attempts to change them as people.

- The strength of character and courage required to live nonviolently elevates the approach above the myth that "turning the other cheek" is just a punk's way out, and that anyone who is nonviolent is simply afraid.

- Presented as both philosophy and methodology, nonviolence "rings true" to many people in management and human service roles. It captures the complexity and texture of everyday work with people by emphasizing the practical value of a positive approach, while not shrinking from the difficulties of dealing with the negative side of human nature.

- Training also allows individuals to begin a potential lifestyle change, not alone, but with a group of people who have shared the training experience. The training is an opportunity for people to make a commitment to a "higher road" with the support of others.

- Many people are surprised to discover that they seem to have been waiting for something like nonviolence to come along. We have been told that the training has energized and given rise to new motivation; that it has transformed how others are viewed; and that it has provided a new framework for thinking about solving problems and managing conflicts.

In conclusion, although we have become strong advocates of this type of training, we try as professional educators and researchers to keep things in perspective. Nonviolence training seems to meet a need, but it must be regarded as a work in progress rather than a finished product. It is a type of intervention that demonstrably has a positive effect on attitudes, knowledge, and skill potential. It also seems adaptable to the needs of many different audiences. As we go forward, we have adopted a "continuous improvement" approach to the further development and evaluation of nonviolence training. We believe that this approach is in keeping with the spirit of nonviolence itself, and with Gandhi's advice to continue experimenting with it.

Chapter 4 - There's More to Nonviolence Than I Thought

"The nonviolent approach does not immediately change the heart of the oppressor. It first does something to the hearts and souls of those committed to it. It gives them new self-respect; it calls up resources of strength and courage that they did not know they had. Finally it reaches the opponent and so stirs his conscience that reconciliation becomes a reality."

Rev. Dr. Martin Luther King, Jr.

On the evening of January 30, 1956 in Montgomery, Alabama, Martin Luther King Jr. stood in front of his home, which had just been bombed.

At the time, he was the leader of the bus boycott, sparked on December 1, 1955 when Rosa Parks refused to give up her seat on a city bus to a white person. The aim of the boycott was to end the city's long-standing official policy of segregating whites and blacks on the city's buses. Facing Dr. King that evening was a crowd of his supporters, angry that their leader's house had been attacked, and especially angry that Mrs. King and the couple's first child, Yolanda, had been placed in danger of losing their lives. Dr. King's friends felt they had plenty of justification to seek revenge. Some of them had brought weapons, and they were ready to retaliate violently against white citizens and their property. All it would take was a word from Martin Luther King.

Dr. King told his friends to go home, and to put away their weapons. He reminded them that their boycott had a great purpose, and that to resort to violence would be to throw all their work away in one instant of madness. He reassured them that he and his family were all right. Somewhat calmed, his followers did as he asked.

In her later recollection of that time, Coretta Scott King picked that night as one of the most important moments of the Civil Rights Movement. The boycott went on to win an important victory in the U.S. Supreme Court, which held that the state and city segregation laws, such as Montgomery's laws requiring segregated buses, were unconstitutional.

Big-Tent Nonviolence

Over the past century, the most famous examples of nonviolence in action have been the campaigns of Mohandas K. Gandhi in India against British colonial rule, and of Martin Luther King, Jr. in the United States to eliminate legalized racial segregation. Nonviolent methods have also been used in opposition to virtually every war of modern times, to the nuclear arms race, to military conscription in many countries, and to many types of economic exploitation and political repression. On another front, the exercise of democratic methods such as voting, and the balance of power among branches of a government can be seen as nonviolent alternatives to violent coercion. So can the rational and humane problem-solving methods of good leaders and managers everywhere. Many of the world's religions and cultures have contributed to the literature of nonviolence. And nonviolence has heroes all over the world, from the

Buddha to Baha'u'llah (founder of the Baha'I faith) and from Danilo Dolci ('the Gandhi of Sicily') to Aung San Suu Kyi (recipient of the Nobel Peace Prize for her opposition to the military rulers of Burma). There are many types and flavors of nonviolence all over the world.

The Montgomery bus boycott was the first of Dr. King's major campaigns aimed at ending the American apartheid of legalized racial segregation in the Southern states, and its success made a profound impression all over the world. Importantly, it was a campaign whose success was built on a deliberate commitment to nonviolence.

The story about Dr. King reminding his angry friends of the path they had chosen to walk with him illustrates the understated power of nonviolence as an approach to solving difficult problems. Turning away from violence not only saved lives that night, but also preserved the credibility and momentum of a historic movement for social change. It drew admiration and support for Dr. King and his cause. And it provided an example of people choosing - consciously, strategically - to get beyond their present desire for revenge in order to win a larger prize.

It is easy to recognize an instance of nonviolence when, as in the story about Dr. King on his porch, a person visibly turns away from violence in a historically important conflict where we might have expected violence to break out. But nonviolence is also at work in situations that are less dramatic. Everyday examples of nonviolence also involve turning away from hostility and enemy-thinking:

- In a dispute between family members, nonviolence could mean finding a time to discuss the issue when the anger has mostly subsided.
- In physically threatening situations, nonviolence could mean trying to talk first rather than fighting or giving in.
- In a business negotiation, nonviolence could mean trying to satisfy the other side's needs as well as your own.
- In parenting, nonviolence could mean showing children how to solve problems in a step-by-step way, teaching respect for others, and modeling the values of patience, humor, and responsibility.
- In political action, nonviolence could mean taking the time to understand the positions, motives, interests, needs, capabilities, and limitations of all the parties involved.
- In dealing with highly volatile community conflicts, nonviolence could mean seeking "win-win" solutions in which everyone's needs and interests are identified and respected.

In all these situations, nonviolence means working with others respectfully and in a spirit of sensible problem solving. The examples above are stated in positive rather than negative language. They use the word "could" - in part to emphasize that we usually have more than one nonviolent option to choose from. In each example, nonviolence would also include avoiding insults and attempts to degrade or humiliate others, as well as, yes, finally, refraining from physical violence.

Nonviolence is a large topic. It is a rich and rewarding subject for study, practice, reflection, sharing with others, and choosing directions for action. Nonviolence is not one "pure" idea. People with diverse points of view can understand it differently. Some people are nonviolent for strictly practical reasons, because they can only get what they want using nonviolent methods. Other people try to live their whole lives nonviolently, because they believe in nonviolence as a basic principle of ethical living. There are also people who are somewhere in between.

Our view in this book is that nonviolence is a "big tent." Within this tent we find a family of approaches that have much in common, are pulling in roughly the same direction, and include a range of applications from the individual to the global. Nonviolence is not a rigid set of dogmatic rules. It is more inclusive than exclusive, and it welcomes creative discussion of nonviolent approaches to both particular problems and living in general.

Five Aspects of Nonviolence

We propose to break nonviolence down into five parts or aspects: opposition to violence, caring about others, goal-orientation, facing reality, and personal investment.
Why are we taking this approach, and why these five aspects?

Over the years, we have introduced nonviolence to many people: students (from elementary school to graduate school), adults in community workshops and churches, and special groups such as prison guards, mental health workers, and teachers. Over and over, people have returned from their

113

first few hours of exploration in nonviolence with such
reactions as these:
"There is more to nonviolence than I thought."
"I thought it was just about 'turning the other cheek,' but
nonviolence is so much more."
"I had no idea of all the other implications."
"Why didn't I have to take a course on this when I was in
school?"

We think that the five aspects of nonviolence discussed
here begin to capture what people mean when they say that
there is "more to nonviolence" than they had expected. And
we have found that almost anyone studying the traditions of
nonviolence soon concludes that these aspects are closely
intertwined. In keeping with our broad, "big tent" approach,
we do not locate nonviolence in any one aspect, but use the
term "nonviolence" to tie all of them together.

1. Opposition to Violence

Ahimsa, the Sanskrit term for noninjury, is one of the
origins of nonviolence, and is of course at the very core of
what people learn from exposure to nonviolence education,
whether in training workshops, school or college courses, or
through reading.
Being opposed to violence is implied by the very word
"nonviolence." What may not be obvious at first is that
opposition to violence itself breaks down into more than one
idea. There are at least three types of opposition to violence
that deserve to be highlighted: (i) not committing violence
ourselves (which comes closest to the root idea of *ahimsa*); (ii)
not cooperating with violence and oppression committed by

others (a twist on *ahimsa* developed by Thoreau, Tolstoy, Gandhi, and others); and (iii) finding alternative, creative ways to respond to violence. This third type of opposition is often the most surprising and rewarding part of opposing violence, and the part that has come to be emphasized by the social sciences and by helping professions such as counseling.

Not Committing Violence Ourselves

There are not very many statements that everyone in the world would agree on. But here is one candidate: "If everyone else were nonviolent, the world would be better than it is now."

Do you agree? Most people do. Would you be willing to go further and include yourself among those who should be nonviolent? Do you sense a bit of hesitation this time? Why?

Most of us commit at least small acts of violence occasionally. When we do, each of us is wired to see our own violence as justified. We say things all the time that reveal this self-justification, such as "She hit me first," "He had it coming," or "I had to teach him a lesson." These statements are not facts but rationalizations for a choice we made to be violent.

Usually when a person commits an act of violence, he or she justifies it in terms of self-protection or self-defense. I might be striking back at you in retaliation because you punched me in the nose. Or I might be part of an army invading your country – just as a precaution, before you can invade my country. Whether it is retaliatory or precautionary,

I probably tell myself that the violence is necessary. It is necessary in order to protect myself from you harming me.

When harm is extended to include disrespect, I can construct a justification for resentment, hostility, and even physical violence in response to almost anything that makes me feel even slightly misused. Disrespect, the great common thread running through all acts of violence, pulls open the door to violence, by making my retaliation feel proper, and even necessary.

Nonviolence asks us to question this way of justifying our own violence. On the one hand, we consciously deplore violence and want to get rid of it: "There is just too much violence in the world today." Yet, almost instinctively, we reserve the right to be violent in our own defense: "But I'll hurt you if you try anything, buddy."

Now, if all violence can be justified in terms of self-defense, we have not moved anywhere. To break out of this pattern of thinking, we need to take responsibility for ending our own violence, acting in ways that discourage violence by others if possible, and looking for means other than violence to protect and defend ourselves.

Making the decision not to commit violence ourselves is very scary for most people. It feels like exposing ourselves to danger. Actually, this decision makes little or no difference in the external dangers that we usually face. However, deciding not to commit violence reduces the danger that we pose to others, and - because people tend to reap what they sow – reduces the likelihood that our behavior will provoke others to violence. Considering all the everyday forms of violence in which we might participate (just think of road rage), the decision not to commit violence ourselves can be an important step toward making our own world safer.

Not Cooperating with Violence Committed by Others

The large-scale violence of British colonial rule in India was the target of several noncooperation campaigns led by Gandhi. For example, in the "Salt Satyagraha" Indians defied the British salt monopoly by refusing to buy British salt and instead making their own. Similarly, Martin Luther King Jr. led campaigns of economic noncooperation against the abusive Jim Crow system of segregated public buses, restrooms, stores, and other public facilities in the southern United States. When these campaigns were illegal under the prevailing laws, they were by definition examples of civil disobedience.

Noncooperation with violence includes more than civil disobedience, however. One achievement of the women's movement over the past generation has been the creation of agencies and shelters where victims of domestic violence and sexual assault can find safety and assistance. The shelters and the movement that created them can be seen as a form of active noncooperation with intimate partner violence - a shameful plague that unfortunately is found all over the world.

The literature on noncooperation with governmental authority includes Henry David Thoreau's famous essay *Civil Disobedience*[31] and the Russian novelist Leo Tolstoy's writings[32] in opposition to militarism and the church's support of conscription under the Czars. The stance of conscientious objection to military service is an important and controversial type of noncooperation, but its more recent stories are little known publicly.[33]

Garden-variety bullying is close to home for most of us. Bullies get away with violence when we passively cooperate with them by remaining silent bystanders. Obviously one active approach would be to fight with the bully, a response of punitive violence. As we know, this is the response that many people advocate and promote.

But a student named Emily in one of our workshops envisioned another active approach. Emily believed that if a large percentage of the people in her high school knew about nonviolence, the peer pressure among students would then operate very differently. She imagined that if a bullying incident occurred in the hallway between classes, a crowd of students might converge immediately, telling the bully that violence is stupid and that the way to earn respect is to show respect. This would be active noncooperation with a common form of violence, but clearly it would require preparation in the form of comprehensive nonviolence education.

Schools should be asking not just how bullies should be punished, but how Emily's crowd of nonviolent students could become a natural feature of the school's culture.

Emily's insight was that, although there are many inspiring stories about individuals responding nonviolently in potentially violent situations, we should not ask individual nonviolence to perform miracles in the midst of a culture that is accustomed to passively cooperating with violence. Rather, we should use nonviolence education to change the culture so that it no longer provides nourishment to violence. For her, and for us, nonviolence training would be a step in that direction.

Creating Alternative Ways to Respond

Nonviolence doesn't work by somehow taking away the option of violence, which many people perceive as their most obvious means of self-defense. Rather, nonviolence seeks to provide better options than violence for achieving happiness and security. One of the pleasures of learning about nonviolence is discovering that there is more - much more - to nonviolence than simply "not using violence." There are hundreds of stories about nonviolence that are marked by moments of surprise, relief, humor, and unexpected discovery, as creative solutions are found to problems that had seemed doomed to violence. Consider this Civil Rights Movement story from David Halberstam's book *The Children*:[34]

The Nashville sit-in campaign of 1960, led by a group of black college students including Bernard LaFayette, the author of our Foreword, was the beginning of desegregation in that city. The nonviolence-trained students were frequently harassed by groups of young white men who resented the changes that were taking place.

One Saturday, a group of students was walking to a lunch counter demonstration when a gang of white men attacked them. A student named Solomon Gort was knocked down and was being beaten. LaFayette moved to protect Gort by covering him with his own body, whereupon the attackers turned their kicks and blows on Bernard.

The person who had been teaching nonviolent strategy to the students was Jim Lawson, a pastor who had come to Nashville at the urging of Martin Luther King precisely because Lawson had spent time in India studying Gandhi's legacy. Lawson calmly walked up to the beating of Gort and LaFayette, and the gang turned its attention to this new person. Lawson, cool and mature, wasn't fighting - but he was clearly interfering with their business.
The leader of the gang spat on Lawson. Lawson remained calm, and asked the leader for a handkerchief. A handkerchief was given, and Lawson wiped the spit off. Then, noting that the leader wore a leather jacket, Lawson asked him if he owned a motorcycle. He did. Some questions and answers about motorcycles followed, while in the background Gort and LaFayette got to their feet and the students resumed their walk. Rejoining the students, Lawson waved at the gang leader, who just remained still, watching them go, and probably wondering what had just happened.

Our colleague Bernard LaFayette went on to join Dr. King's staff, and has become a beloved nonviolence educator in the King tradition. He was one of the eight "Children" who are the main focus of Halberstam's book about several young people who became first foot soldiers, and later veterans, of the Civil Rights Movement.

We will always be deeply moved by Jim Lawson's courage and creativity in the "motorcycle story." To us, this story is a good example of how nonviolence includes much more than just refraining from violence, and how it often involves surprise - a departure from the violent script that people have been expecting events to follow.

A key idea in the practice of nonviolence is that every situation offers us a range of ways in which to respond. Usually, some of these options will be more in the spirit of nonviolence than others, and so we can choose a response from the more nonviolent end of this spectrum. We may have difficulty seeing the range of options arrayed before us, perhaps because we have formed strong habits to respond in only one standard way. However, we can learn to see a wider range of options through study, discussion, openness to ideas that are not obvious, and sheer practice. For many people, it is a big step forward just to begin thinking about the existence of this range of options.

However, finding alternatives to violence does not necessarily depend on a head-scratching random brainstorming of logical possibilities. In the motorcycle story, it is important that Jim Lawson's way of transforming the danger of violence into a less threatening situation involved focusing on a human connection between adversaries. We can generalize from this example to say that many stories of nonviolence are stories about relationship-building. We can be pretty certain that the alternatives most likely to transform conflict peacefully are those that focus on human relationships.

2. Caring About Others

Increased caring about others is an outcome of nonviolence education that relates directly to the origin concept *agape*. Let's examine some of the ways in which caring manifests itself, and some of the specific obstacles to be overcome.

Author Charles Collyer, together with Abu Bakr, a nonviolence trainer and formerly Assistant to the President of the University of Rhode Island, devised an informal scale for rating the atmosphere in schools they visited. At the bottom of the scale were schools where, from the teachers and administrators, we would hear things like this: "These damn kids. They won't listen to a word you say. You can't turn your back on them. You guys better watch out. They'll manipulate you." At the other extreme were schools where we would hear things like this: "These are our kids. It's difficult for them these days. But they are good people. Listen to what they have to say. If you respect them, they will listen to you." What do you think it is like to be a student in schools at the top, and at the bottom, of this scale?

We can also imagine a scale that gives a rough measure of how much people care for other people in general. At the bottom would be sentiments like "Don't be a sucker. You can't trust anybody. People are no damn good." At the top would be "Human beings are endlessly fascinating, complex, and wonderful. We have our problems, but just look at what we can do, especially when we work together."

A friend of ours, the blues historian and musician James "Sparky" Rucker, points out that people have two eyes at the front of our heads, rather than one in front and one in back, or one on each side. This means, according to Sparky, that "we can't watch our own backs, so we were meant to look out for each other." Sparky, the gruff old blues guy, is at the top of our caring scale.

Some people really enjoy and like other people, and others do not. It is easier to teach the knowledge and skills of nonviolence to people who have a positive attitude toward others and believe in their potential to be friends and allies. Such people start their own pilgrimage to nonviolence with a head start, because they already possess something that the best teachers of nonviolence always try to encourage.

Both Gandhi and King repeatedly spoke of human beings in a way that emphasized their positive potential. For example,

From Gandhi: "It is the law of love that rules mankind. Had violence [or hate] ruled us, we should have become extinct long ago. And yet the tragedy of it is that the so-called civilized men and nations conduct themselves as if the basis of society was violence. [35]

From King: "…man is neither innately good nor is he innately bad; he has potentialities for both."[36]

Notice that Gandhi and King are not saying that all people are good, period. They are saying that people are capable of both good and bad, and can choose love, justice, nonviolence, and goodness over their opposites.

Can learning about nonviolence improve my attitude toward other people? Evaluations of nonviolence training suggest that the answer is yes. More research needs to be done on this, but the process seems to work as follows:

Nonviolence seeks to find and support what is good in me. That support can make me feel good about myself, and give my self-respect a boost. Nonviolence also points out what is good in you. It can remind me that you deserve my respect too. It can motivate both of us to get to know each other, join forces to get bigger jobs done, find our common problems and work on them together, and help each other when one of us is down. In short, nonviolence leads us to care about each other by focusing attention on the positive common ground that we share with each other.

What prevents many of us from caring for others in this way? There are several forces that can work either for or against caring, including: cultural messages; how we build our identity; how we process our experiences with others; and our world-view or religion.

Cultural Messages

Many cultural messages support the opposite of caring. For the most part, our culture tells us to care for good people, but to punish bad people. So, before we care about other human beings, we are expected to decide which ones are good and which are bad. Many TV shows, movies, and video games encourage this perception of people as either good or bad. In a typical action movie, the villain is painted as unforgivably bad, and the audience builds up hatred and fear toward (usually) him. Then toward the end of the movie, when an avenging good guy is finally unleashed to make the bad guy suffer, the audience experiences this revenge as justice.

"Well," you might say, "some people commit bad deeds. Isn't it naïve to care about them? Won't that just reward and support more bad deeds?" Let us be clear that people who commit bad deeds must be held accountable for them. Nonviolence and responsibility are emphatically "joined at the hip." But nonviolence requires that we distinguish between two kinds of response: (1) holding others accountable for their behavior, and (2) acting out our own feelings toward them. The first is a proper basis for justice; the second is often anger-driven and irresponsible.

A caring and responsible attitude toward wrongdoers would make punishments fit the crime, avoiding personal injury and humiliation, and providing for as much restoration of damage and rehabilitation as possible. The goal should be to find and develop the best potential for good, not simply to satisfy our temporary craving for revenge. In a great deal of media entertainment however, revenge is equated with justice, and the idea of turning offenders into productive members of the community is barely considered.

It is one thing to be realistically prepared for self-serving and manipulative actions by others. People are not perfect, and we owe it to ourselves to avoid being abused. However, it is easy to go further and, forgetting all the good that can also be drawn out of people, conclude that suspicion should dominate our attitude toward others. A general good will toward others can coexist with reasonable precautions against abuse. We should consider how cultural messages can be created that would encourage this balance.

How We Build Our Identity

A colleague of ours, a college professor, had a disturbing experience. He had just finished a section of his course on the topic of tensions between different ethnic groups in American society, and had asked his students to write brief comments in reaction to this topic. One student wrote that she felt it was necessary for her to hate some other ethnic groups in order for her to "know myself as a member of my own group." This story suggests that identity, the sense of who we are, is defined not only in terms of positive characteristics that belong to us, but in terms of negative characteristics that are ascribed to others. Why would a person feel less well known to herself without someone to hate? The answer may lie in a commonplace but very powerful bit of human psychology:

The people, places, and things that we experience repeatedly, first become familiar to us, and eventually what is familiar comes to seem normal and even natural. When we encounter new people from backgrounds different than our own, and experience them - their speech, their customs, their most noticeable departures from what is familiar - as "not normal," it is then just a small step to become wary, suspicious, and prejudiced against them, because their unfamiliarity leaves us in a state of uncertainty about what to expect from them. In this almost automatic way, we can develop a collection of contrasting beliefs about Them (the strange, abnormal ones) and Us (the familiar, normal ones) that become part of our identity, our conception of who we are. We are clean; they are dirty. We are intelligent; they are stupid. We know how to behave; they don't. And so on. These thoughts about Them become excuses not to care about Them as fellow human beings, to further distance ourselves from Them, and therefore to crystallize our ignorance and unfamiliarity with Them. To fill the void, we may generate additional poorly grounded beliefs about Them that further distance Them and draw the boundaries between Them and Us even more sharply. This is a vicious cycle in which ignorance and false beliefs feed on each other.

Is there another way to build our identity, other than through negative contrasts with others? Certainly. First, we can be aware of how the experience-familiarity-normality chain works to create our prejudices. Many of the beliefs we arrive at are not objective facts about Them, but products of this chain and related thought processes.

Second, we can counteract these beliefs through better educating ourselves about the world outside our familiar sphere. Good information gathering will reveal that within any group of Them, there is tremendous variation among individuals. Once this is understood, it will render any blanket statements about whole ethnic or racial groups nonsensical.

Third, we can use these tools - awareness of our own thought processes, and meaningful education - to build our own identity on a solid foundation of knowledge about our own strengths and weaknesses, without lazily leaning on shallow overall comparisons with other groups.

How We Process Our Experiences with Others

We all have bad experiences with people. We all have good experiences too. However, memory and attention are selective. It is very easy to select our bad experiences to dwell on, and ignore the good ones. When we do this, we predictably shape our own attitude and mood to be persistently negative. This can set self-fulfilling prophecies into motion, in which the reactions we create through our bad attitude come back to us in the form of hostility and avoidance by other people. What stronger confirmation of our negative views could we get than the nasty hostility of our neighbors and co-workers? And yet, the source of that hostility was not in them, but in our own choice to focus on our own bad experiences. One consequence of this vicious cycle is that we come to care little for others, because we perceive them to be causing our own pain.

Selectivity and self-fulfilling prophecies work in the other direction too. If we select our best experiences with people to think about, that will influence our mood, speech, and actions in a positive way. And what goes around, comes around. Projecting a positive attitude usually influences the people around us to return the favor. It is then pretty easy to care about the welfare of those people, because they are being so good to us!

A balanced view of life recognizes that both good and bad things happen. It also recognizes that our own actions can become good or bad events in the lives of others as well as our own. (How often have I, through carelessness or otherwise, been a part of what someone else experiences as "Murphy's

Law" - the proposition that whatever can go wrong, will go wrong?) There is much more to be said about all this. For the present, however, it is sufficient to note that our willingness to care for others is related to what we select and emphasize in processing our experiences with others.

World View or Religion

Liberating as it is to "let it go" and turn a problem over to a "higher power," this shift to the supernatural can also relieve us of our responsibility to others, and diminish caring about what happens in this world. The Serenity Prayer, attributed to Reinhold Niebuhr and widely used in self-help organizations such as Alcoholics Anonymous, expresses our need for a balance between accepting and acting: "Grant me the serenity to accept the things I cannot change, the courage to change the things I can, and the wisdom to know the difference." Too much emphasis on the first part can hold us back from caring. Too much emphasis on the second can make us a loose cannon. It really does take wisdom to know the difference.

Both Gandhi and King were religious men, but in a worldly way that made them different from some of the other leaders of their religions. Gandhi directed his Hindu followers away from supernatural fatalism. He emphasized what people could do in this life to free themselves and improve conditions for women and the "untouchables." King criticized other Christian ministers who emphasized getting to heaven upon death over improving social conditions for the living.

Like cultural messages, the building of identity, and the processing of our own experiences, our world-view or religion can either promote or inhibit caring for others. Learning about nonviolence nudges a person in the direction of caring, and so may transform how each of these factors operates in our lives.

3. Goal Orientation

We can analyze Goal-Orientation into at least two important ideas. One is the concept expressed beautifully in the phrase "Eyes on the Prize" — that we should resist being sidetracked in the pursuit of our most important goals; the other is the requirement that, in solving problems, our methods should be consistent with the goals we are pursuing.

Eyes on the Prize

The wonderful phrase "Eyes on the Prize" is the title of a video history of the Civil Rights Movement, produced by the Public Broadcasting System. The phrase comes from the determined refrain of the gospel freedom song "Hold On." Here is the last verse of the familiar Alice Wine version:

> Got my hand on the freedom plow,
> Wouldn't take nothin' for my journey now.
> Keep your eyes on the prize, hold on.
> Hold on, hold on!
> Keep your eyes on the prize, hold on.

Keeping our eyes on the prize means staying focused on our main goal. That is what Martin Luther King was doing that January evening in 1956 when he asked his angry friends to go home. This kind of goal orientation is the opposite of an automatic reflex; it is a skill, a way of thinking that must be learned. Stories like the one about Dr. King can help us to cultivate this skill and bring it closer to being our habitual way of operating.

In nonviolence, the skill of staying focused on what is really important is called upon when we must survive moments of anger which threaten to lead us into insulting, threatening, humiliating, or physically hurting others. These moments usually pass, and are followed by a calmer emotional state in which we are less inclined to hurt our "enemy" and more able to work nonviolently to solve our problems with him or her.

The song "Hold On" is part of the rich musical heritage of the Civil Rights Movement and its precursors. Its message - be patient, keep working for good, and keep the goal in mind - was a needed reminder to people who were assaulted daily by the taunts, cruelty, and abuse of the powerful, for years and years.

Actually, both King and Gandhi were often criticized for their patience in the face of this abuse. People are easily tempted into lashing back at those who hurt them. But in the long run, it became clear that the patience of these great leaders was a purposeful, restrained choice about how to respond. Their reputations were built by pressing a long-term struggle against injustice while refusing to be baited into short-term violence.

The old advice about moments of anger, that we should "count to ten" (or a hundred) in order to let anger pass, is good advice. But we should also understand that getting through these moments is not done just to demonstrate that we can do it. Staying under control helps us to achieve our goals. The advice would be more complete if it said "count to ten, and while you do, keep your eyes on the prize."

Consistency of Methods and Goals

Another theme that runs through both Gandhi's and Martin Luther King's writings is that our means (that is, our methods) should be consistent with our ends (that is, our goals). More exactly,

" ... nonviolence demands that the means we use must be as pure as the ends we seek." [37]

Now, think about this. Is Dr. King saying that "the end justifies the means"?

No, quite the contrary. The phrase "the end justifies the means" suggests that there is only one moral decision to make - that after we have chosen a good goal, any method for achieving it is then justified. But Dr. King is not saying that at all. Instead, he is saying that we need to make two moral decisions, not just one, and both must be good decisions. We must choose both our ends and our means. Furthermore, we need to choose each of them nonviolently, so that the consistency achieved is one in which the means and the ends do not poison and undermine each other. The goodness of one component does not automatically carry over to the other, as implied by the "end justifies the means" claim. But badness does carry over. We can undermine a good goal by choosing evil methods to attain it. And the surface goodness of our methods will be undermined if we use them to pursue an evil goal.

The consistency of methods and goals is another high standard to which nonviolence holds us. The benefits that flow from consistency include, first, the quality of a person's reputation. A person who is recognized as being of good character is often one whose methods and goals are consistent with each other. Second, and perhaps more important, is that goals achieved through consistent nonviolent methods are not burdened with an embarrassing history of underhanded methods. They are more likely to be goals we can be proud of, and to be longer lasting.

An obvious objection must be stated: Our very ability to choose nonviolent methods is sometimes limited because of a past history of hostile actions and persistent avoidance of nonviolent problem-solving. For example, the Treaty of Versailles ending World War I was a punitive treaty that humiliated Germany and so bred resentment in that country against the Allies, fueling "enemy thinking" rather than defusing it. The failure to end World War I in a fair and compassionate way led twenty years later to World War II. It is commonly said that for the Allies, fighting World War II was necessary, because the goal of defeating Hitler was so important. Indeed, World War II does seem to be a case where the end justified the means, and is often used as an argument against nonviolence in general. What is often forgotten is that the violent means of war would not have been necessary if the problem represented by Hitler had been addressed through more pragmatic and less vindictive diplomacy twenty years earlier.

A great reason to practice nonviolence all the time, and not just in times of crisis, is to stay off the slippery slope that leads individuals and nations into violent conflict as the lesser of available evils.

(Paradoxically, the prevention of war escapes our attempts to study it, because what is prevented, by definition, never presents itself for study. This is a familiar dilemma for those who argue the merits of prevention in many domains of problem-solving - poverty, crime, public health, and the environment, to name a few.)

A more immediate and positive motive for practicing nonviolence all of the time is that everyday life is then more productive, satisfying, and fun. Happily, these benefits can be measured. And, incidentally, this kind of life prevents violence.

Of course, we must also be prepared for crisis, and for the use of extreme means if necessary. But we should not depend on creating violent man-made crises to keep us energized and ready to use these capabilities; there are always plenty of naturally occurring crises to do that. We should base our preparation and training on a realistic view of the world and of human nature, recognizing that however much we may wish for a placid existence with no crises, wishing alone won't make it real. The actual world in which we must live and take part ironically often forces us into struggle to achieve peace and freedom.

So, after achieving any measure of peace and freedom, it is unwise to relax, congratulate ourselves, and just coast. "Freedom isn't free," we hear politicians say. True. However, yet another irony is that this slogan is often used to justify wars that could have been prevented at much lower cost — prevented by acting in accordance with that very same slogan. A fair price for freedom is eternal nonviolent vigilance.

4. Facing Reality

The expression "facing reality" typically evokes one of two interpretations. It could be understood as passively accepting the real world with resignation, as in the remark, "You may as well face reality …" Or it could be understood as actively confronting the world as it really is, in order to solve real problems, instead of indulging in wishful thinking.

Here we are interested in the second, more active sense of "facing reality." Let us break this aspect of nonviolence into three components: acquiring accurate knowledge; facing unpleasant as well as pleasant facts; and adopting practical strategies and tactics.

Acquiring Accurate Knowledge

Nonviolence aims to create a better world. However, you can't improve something unless you have accurate knowledge about its current condition - that is, about its reality. In his *Letter from Birmingham Jail*, Martin Luther King said that the first step in any nonviolent campaign is "the collection of facts to determine whether injustices exist." In a larger sense, information gathering is the first responsibility of anyone who hopes to solve a problem.

There are typically two kinds of knowledge that we need: general background to build our understanding of the context, and specific information about the problem at hand.

We also need to have a good understanding of nonviolence itself, including its history, its philosophical variations, and a broad repertoire of examples. We need to understand human nature as well as possible, and with as much generosity and tolerance as we can muster. We need to know how the world works economically, politically, and technically, the pitfalls and problems that people can face, and ways of bringing help to bear. And we need to understand artistic expression - how people tell in language and music and visual images about the human condition.

These are reasons to commit to a life of continual learning and education. They are offered to anyone who is looking for a reason to stay in school, go back to school, to study research methods, or to start in on the study of a worthwhile subject.

Facing Unpleasant as well as Pleasant Facts

A practitioner of nonviolence should not be naïve. The world includes very harsh and unpleasant realities. The arenas in which nonviolence is most needed are environments in which ugly things happen. Women fear bodily injury and death at the hands of current and former lovers. High school students are victimized by bullying, drugs, gambling, and sexual predation. Gangs retaliate against each other in brutal ambushes. Co-workers manipulate and sabotage each other for advantage in the workplace. Salespeople tell outright lies dozens of times each day to maintain their incomes and their jobs. Arms dealers sell deadly weapons to both sides in wars around the world. This dreary and disgraceful list goes on and on.

There is no quick remedy for most of these problems. Nonviolence does not assume that we can solve difficult problems quickly, or that violent people can be turned around with just a few words. It does offer some insights however:

- Violence tends to occur as part of a cycle of mutual retaliation which we need to understand if we are to interrupt it.
- Likewise, violence especially pervades systems in which some people oppress and intimidate others.
- The perpetrators of violence are degraded by their own actions, and so suffer losses which we need to appreciate.
- The positive common ground that people share is easily pushed aside and forgotten in conflict. This loss of connection happens without conscious intent. However, re-establishing common ground takes deliberate effort and skill.
- In most conflicts, each side owns part of the truth. That is, each has a perspective on the problem that is rooted in real interests and needs. Therefore, we need to learn from both sides, even when some of the truth may be embedded in grave injustices.

Nonviolent leaders are sometimes criticized for their willingness to attribute some truths, some value, to an enemy hated by their followers. But one of the ways in which people avoid reality is by refusing to learn from people who are disliked and despised. We can obviously learn more if we do not avoid any information that can help us solve difficult problems.

Adopting Practical Strategies and Tactics

Gandhi and King were both skilled politicians. They made shrewd judgments every day about all the practical needs of their movements. They picked their battles carefully. They built support for difficult political tasks by bringing people from different classes and interest groups together. Their success was grounded in facing the facts of each situation and working with the real interests and limitations of the people who were involved. The changes they brought about could not have been accomplished if these leaders had been naïve or impractical men.

However, in a critique of Gandhi's nonviolence, the theologian Reinhold Niebuhr (whom King greatly admired) made a distinction between Gandhi's attempts to deal with others out of a spirit of good will, and his political methods. He described the first as a loving attitude:

"Non-violence, for him, has really become a term by which he expresses the ideal of love, the spirit of moral goodwill. This involves for him freedom from personal resentments and a moral purpose, free of selfish ambition. It is the temper and spirit in which a political policy is conducted ... rather than a particular political technique." [38]

Physically nonviolent political action, however, like violent methods, according to Niebuhr, is not neutral but coercive:

"Non-violent coercion and resistance, in short, is a type of coercion which offers the largest opportunities for a harmonious relationship with the moral and rational factors in social life." [39]

Though the young Martin Luther King was at first somewhat taken aback by Niebuhr's characterization of nonviolence as a form of coercion, he was definitely inspired by the conclusion of Niebuhr's argument (written 25 years before the Montgomery Bus Boycott) as it related to black people in America:

"This means that non-violence is a particularly strategic instrument for an oppressed group which is hopelessly in the minority and has no possibility of developing sufficient power to set against its oppressors. The emancipation of the Negro race in America probably waits upon the adequate development of this kind of social and political strategy. It is hopeless for the Negro to expect complete emancipation from the menial social and economic position into which the white man has forced him, merely by trusting in the moral sense of the white race. It is equally hopeless to attempt emancipation through violent rebellion." [40]

Both as a student and throughout his career, King must have read this prophetic passage of Niebuhr's again and again.

Was nonviolence used coercively by Gandhi, and later by King? The short answer must be yes. Nonviolence has often been used to pressure political and economic powers to "do the right thing." Consider this passage from the *Letter from Birmingham Jail*, written by a more seasoned Dr. King:

"You may well ask: 'Why direct action? Why sit-ins, marches, and so forth? Isn't negotiation a better path?' You are quite right in calling for negotiation. Indeed this is the very purpose of direct action. Nonviolent direct action seeks to create such a crisis and foster such a tension that a community which has constantly refused to negotiate is forced to confront the issue. It seeks so to dramatize the issue that it can no longer be ignored. My citing the creation of tension as part of the work of the nonviolent resister may sound rather shocking. But I must confess that I am not afraid of the word 'tension.' I have earnestly opposed violent tension, but there is a type of constructive, nonviolent tension which is necessary for growth." [41]

Here we see clearly King's view of nonviolence as a strong and active force, capable of grappling with difficult real-world problems. This view contrasts sharply with the assumption held by many people that nonviolence is a passive or resigned attitude, averse to tension or confrontation.

The strategies and tactics of nonviolence have, for the most part, been developed by disadvantaged people. Its practitioners – in South Africa, India, the United States, the

Philippines, Chile, and many other places - were not able to get what they wanted by physical force, great wealth, or raw political power. So they devised ways for relatively powerless people to exert pressure for change in other ways. The invention of nonviolent political action deserves a place in any list of examples of human progress.

5. Personal Investment

Personal investment means the effort and time and sacrifice that each of us puts in to become more nonviolent. Like nonviolence itself, personal investment takes many forms and is related to many other ideas. Let us approach this aspect of nonviolence by considering first the goals of personal investment, and then the methods that move us toward these goals.

Goals

There are two broad goals of personal investment: (1) personal development or empowerment, and (2) becoming a more effective agent of social change. There is actually some conflict between those who emphasize personal empowerment as an outcome of nonviolence, and those who see such empowerment as secondary to, and even a distraction from, the goal of agency for social change. We regard both personal development and agency for social change as worthwhile goals. Each provides a good reason for personal investment, and there is no necessary reason for them to be in conflict with each other. Rather, they should complement each other.

Almost all supporters of nonviolence would agree that individual human beings have an obligation to be instruments of positive change. To become more effective instruments, they should make a personal investment of time and energy to learn and practice the skills of nonviolence. The personal investment itself can be rewarding, and so can become one of the attractions of nonviolence. Many good programs for youth, including nonviolence training programs, can promise greater pride, confidence, and a sense of empowerment as beneficial outcomes.

Ironically, it is also desirable for a practitioner of nonviolence to be capable of violence. To abstain from violence only because one is too weak to use it, doesn't really count as nonviolence. Better is to be capable of violence, but choose nonviolent options deliberately and consistently. Therefore, one goal of personal development can be to become strong in the ways usually associated with violence. For example, martial arts training, especially in philosophically nonviolent disciplines such as aikido, has been chosen by many individuals as part of their personal investment in nonviolence.[42]

There is room for a great deal of variation in the goals adopted by different individuals. In a living tradition like nonviolence, we think it is quite proper for tastes and preferences to come into play. Also, life is not long enough to become a master of every skill, field of knowledge, art, or vocation. The value we place on personal growth itself, and the process of growing toward our goals, are more important than the particular discipline or level of skill we may attain.

Methods

Personal investment should probably include a daily program or regimen, in which development toward our goals receives some deliberate attention. Some people are naturally inclined toward such programs, and are strict about them. Others are more casual. Again, there is room for variation.

Gandhi is the most famous example of a nonviolent leader trying to practice everything he preached, starting with his own personal choices and routines. In Gandhi's case, personal investment took the form of giving up material possessions, alcohol, meat, sex, and many ordinary sources of comfort. His fasts, originally undertaken to put political pressure on his followers and opponents, also became a voluntary form of personal self-purification. He believed that his own life would inevitably be viewed as an example to others of nonviolence. Therefore, he wanted to ensure that people could learn about nonviolence by observing him. He also wanted to gain the political advantage of being seen as a poor and humble citizen-leader.

However, he had a wonderful sense of humor about the symbolic side of his asceticism: in the movie <u>Gandhi</u> we hear his acknowledgment that it cost a great deal of his supporters' money to keep him in poverty!

Many people, using Gandhi as their example, recoil from the self-sacrifice that they assume nonviolence requires. But, in fact, there are no "nonviolence police" out there checking up on our degrees of personal investment to ensure that they are adequate! Supporters of nonviolence cover quite a wide range on the dimension of personal investment, from relatively high, such as Gandhi-like self-denial, to relatively low, such as simply holding positive attitudes toward nonviolence among those whose lifestyles are more typical.

Reading about nonviolence, talking about it with others, and devoting time to hands-on applications of nonviolence, are all forms of personal investment that are accessible and worthwhile. Spending time in these ways has the direct benefit of building our understanding. It also brings the indirect benefit of enriching the rest of our time. As the saying goes, "What's not to like?"

In Conclusion

We have examined five aspects of nonviolence - five varieties of discovery that we have observed in people who are learning about the details of nonviolence for the first time. One of the aspects - opposition to violence - is couched in a semantically negative way. The other four - caring for others, goal-orientation, facing reality, and personal investment - are couched positively.

In the end, the positive or negative phrasing of these aspects when briefly stated, is their least important feature. It is clear to everyone who does a little study that nonviolence is a positive and powerful concept. However, the negative valence of the term nonviolence itself may be partly responsible for the relatively poor understanding that so many people have of this powerful idea.

There is nothing fixed or sacred about the five aspects of nonviolence presented here. The purpose of discussing these aspects has simply been to stimulate your interest in nonviolence by opening up and laying out some of its richness for inspection.

When Dr. King spoke to his followers after the bombing of his home in Montgomery, he personified nonviolence for them, and dramatically turned them away from committing violence. His example broadened their view of nonviolence, and ultimately confirmed for the crowd that Dr. King's approach was the one they wanted.
Consider what it must have been like to be a member of that crowd of angry friends. That was a real, powerful moment in time for them. Their emotions ran high. Before Dr. King spoke to them, they were about to go out and repeat a mistake that vengeful people have made millions of times before in human history, a mistake that has usually resulted only in further hostility and destruction. But in that moment, the crowd heard a voice of reason, compassion, and quietly confident leadership, using that very moment to guide them and to teach a critically important lesson. That moment made all the difference. The world needs more moments turned to good purpose like that one. If more people become educated in nonviolent problem-solving, there will be more of us who are able to do what Dr. King did that night.

Nonviolence has multiple though related facets, and can challenge a person with its unfamiliarity as well as its complexity, its scariness, its combination of idealism and practicality, its connection to many different problems and fields, its applicability to difficult problems, and its very colorful literature.

We hope you will discover more about nonviolence through further exploration, and then - most importantly - pass on this understanding to others.

Chapter 5 - Making Nonviolence Real

One often hears the criticism that nonviolence is commendably idealistic, but not realistic. So this chapter is concerned with realism. To what extent can nonviolence be made real in the world, and what does it look like when it is realized?

We have presented many examples of nonviolence and approximations to nonviolence throughout *Discovering Nonviolence* and its companion, *Agape and Ahimsa*. We hope that these examples and approximations have provided a glimpse of the inclusive or "big tent" conception of nonviolence. We hope readers will see in these cases a kind of nonviolence that is robust and practical in real life.

However, there are two "reality issues" that we should discuss more fully and directly. One is a concern of scientists and policy makers: the issue of measurable outcomes. The other is a concern of professions charged with using force: the practicality of nonviolence in the face of violent threats.

Measurable Outcomes

For the most part, when we have spoken of the "outcomes" of nonviolence in this book, we have meant changed attitudes toward other people and toward problem-solving. We have described these changes in words and stories rather than in statistical terms. For most social scientists, however, the measurability of outcomes is paramount. And in the disciplines concerned with human services and organizational development there is a branch of applied social science called program evaluation, which uses rigorous methodology to test for the existence of real effects of educational and other programs. This book is not a guide to research on the effects of nonviolence education. However, abundant research does exist in fields such as psychology and education, and advanced study in nonviolence should include this literature. There are studies of the basic psychological processes that underlie aggressive and prosocial behavior. There are also applied "outcome studies" in which the impact of specific programs and interventions is documented. This research is rich in ideas related to nonviolence and evidence for the effectiveness of nonviolence education broadly construed. The research literature is too large to be reviewed in this book, but we would like to offer some entry points to this information that we believe will make an immediate connection for the reader between our account of nonviolence and empirical research. Here are some suggestions:

A classic paper on children's imitation of aggressive behavior was published by Albert Bandura and colleagues.[43] This study demonstrated that children would copy the behavior and the words of an adult role model who was observed punching and yelling at an inflatable "Bobo doll." Young children were more likely to imitate if the role model was of their own gender, and boys were overall more aggressive than girls. The study was of theoretical importance because the researchers did not provide obvious rewards to the children for engaging in aggressive behavior. Rather, the children picked up the behavior simply by watching. Many research studies by psychologists followed, examining aspects

148

of modeling and imitation, including the effects of watching violence on television. Bandura's famous Bobo doll study serves here as an example of important research on the basic conditions and psychological processes involved in problematic violent behavior.

A review article by David Johnson and his brother Roger Johnson provides an example of scholarship focused on the effectiveness of programs to reduce violence.[44] These authors reviewed the available literature on conflict resolution and peer mediation programs in schools. They concluded that, while the research was incomplete and problematic, several conclusions could be drawn:

a. Conflicts among students do occur frequently in schools (although the conflicts only rarely result in serious injury).

b. Untrained students by and large use conflict strategies that create destructive outcomes by ignoring the importance of their ongoing relationships.

c. Conflict resolution and peer mediation programs do seem to be effective in teaching students integrative negotiation and mediation procedures.

d. After training, students tend to use these conflict strategies, which generally leads to more constructive outcomes.

e. Students' success in resolving their conflicts constructively tends to reduce the number of student-student conflicts referred to teachers and administrators, which in turn, tends to reduce suspensions.

Johnson and Johnson focused on conflict resolution and peer mediation programs, which we place under the "big

149

tent" of nonviolence education programs. What about programs with other labels and vocabularies for putting what we call nonviolence into practice? Daniel Goleman, in his book *Emotional Intelligence*, provides an appendix called "Social and Emotional Learning: Results."[45] In it he identifies several nonviolence-like programs which have had empirically validated outcomes, with source references. The concerns addressed by these programs include child development, social competence, awareness, problem-solving, and resolving conflict creatively.

One study that directly examined the impact of Kingian nonviolence training on the knowledge and attitudes of several groups who participated in two-day workshops, was done by Maram Hallak in 2000. Dr. Hallak found changes in knowledge and attitudes that lasted for months after the workshops.[46]

Another study showed that brief nonviolence training increases a person's sensitivity to violence, defined as how violent the person considers each of several violent behaviors to be.[47] Even the mere suggestion that an act of violence was justified or unjustified can, under some conditions, change how violent it is considered to be, illustrating how malleable human perceptions of violence are.[48] There are marked individual differences in baseline levels of sensitivity to violence.[49] However, changes in sensitivity are possible for both more sensitive and less sensitive individuals. Reasonably enough, nonviolence is associated with higher levels of awareness of the harm done by both outright violence and by lower levels of mean-spirited behavior.

We believe that these studies reflect a basic truth about teaching peaceful problem-solving: that nonviolence works.

Its effectiveness has been demonstrated over and over again in the research literature. One approach to demonstrating a program's effectiveness is called meta-analysis, in which a systematic review of many research studies is undertaken. In this approach, a large number of studies on a type of treatment are collected, and the results are pooled statistically to create a more powerful test of the treatment's effect. Mark Lipsey and David Wilson carried out a meta-analysis that demonstrated the effectiveness of several kinds of psychological, educational, and behavioral treatments using a variety of outcome measures. To cite only some of the results related to nonviolence education, the paper documents effects in such categories as primary prevention education programs, social skills training, social learning treatment and diversion programs for juvenile delinquents, training in interpersonal cognitive problem-solving skills for children, assertiveness training, and guidance and counseling programs. The treatment effects in these categories were found to be moderate in size - not huge, but not trivial either. In other words, these are programs worth designing, investing in, and implementing; however, they should not be expected to produce dramatic or immediate change in every individual.[50]

A later review of over 200 socio-emotional learning (SEL) programs involving more than a quarter of a million school children, confirmed that SEL promotes not only positive social and emotional behavior but higher academic achievement.[51] (The emergence of good measures of SEL effects has tempted some school systems to begin using these measures not as tools to encourage progress in character development, but high-stakes tests to rank schools and punish low-performing teachers. Angela Duckworth, a leading researcher on SEL and character development, is among those

151

resisting this more "violent" application of our new knowledge about the importance of nonviolence.)[52]

A great many other studies could be cited. The research supporting nonviolence education constitutes a strong empirical foundation for the development of programs aimed at teaching the skills of nonviolence. In a way, the social science research community has followed Gandhi's advice to experiment with nonviolence, to refine it and develop it further. Of course, we still need to translate what we know about nonviolence more fully into real life. And we need to keep studying and experimenting with new ways to create peace, and to train future generations to continue this work.

Nonviolence in the Face of Violent Threats

The attacks of September 11, 2001 set off a great many discussions about how people should respond to violence. The attacks were extreme, and the deliberate killing of innocent people has been almost universally condemned – a tragic point of agreement throughout the months and years of public debate. There was also a general agreement – so general that it is rarely stated – that people want their leaders' responses to terrorism to make the situation better rather than worse. However, people have disagreed over whether particular responses, such as military counterattack, or specific forms of counterattack, are necessary or unnecessary, and whether they would actually make things better or worse.

Shortly after September 11, there were several sharp criticisms of nonviolence from commentators who took the position that the attacks provided a clear instance in which violent counterattack was justified, and where a nonviolent approach would obviously be inadequate. These commentators made the usual assumption that "nonviolence" means a passive acceptance of wrongdoing. Given that the acknowledged icons of nonviolence, Gandhi and King, gave us powerful examples of how to strike down injustice, it is remarkable that this assumption persists. We trust that readers of this book now understand that real nonviolence vigorously seeks alternatives to both violence and passivity in the face of threats, conflicts, and frustrating problems in general. As Walter Wink has said, it is a third path. Nonviolence is a way of facing reality rather than avoiding it or lashing out.

The authors of this book share the disdain for passivity expressed by those commentators who, we feel mistakenly, set out after September 11 to protect the world from nonviolence. However, as teachers of active nonviolence, the post-attack debates placed us under considerable pressure to explain our position. The pressure has come from both those whose readiness to resort to violence is high, and from others who simply hold the familiar misconceptions of what nonviolence is all about.

There is an approach to the justification of violence, called Just War Theory (JWT), which is often cited as setting limits on nonviolence by saying when war is justified. Let us offer a perspective on JWT from the viewpoint of nonviolence. Then we will consider how a commitment to nonviolence can be brought into several very difficult areas of application. Our aim is to show how nonviolence would look, and sometimes does look, in the real world.

Just War Theory proposes conditions under which a country is justified in going to war. Scaled down, it addresses the more general question of when a person is justified in using force to solve a problem.

JWT proposes that war is justified under the following conditions: it is fought by a legitimate authority; it is fought for a just cause; it is fought as a last resort after other alternatives have been exhausted; and it is fought by ethical means. JWT also includes the traditional principles of discrimination and proportionality. Discrimination means that military personnel and resources, but not innocent civilians, may be targeted for attack. In warfare, imperfect discrimination is acknowledged to lead to some civilian casualties, a result euphemistically called collateral damage. Too much collateral damage may be considered "out of proportion" in any particular action, or for a war as a whole. Proportionality calls for the unwelcome judgment of how much damage is acceptable and how much is unacceptable. It can be seen that JWT offers a weighing of costs and benefits, both for war itself and for actions within a war.[53]

Another way to view JWT is that it is one approach to the setting of a threshold for violence. If a person or country has a low threshold, they will fight their perceived adversary on very little provocation. If the threshold is higher, this means that they would need to be provoked more strongly, or that they would wait longer before engaging in violence against their adversary. The existence of thresholds for violence, which vary from person to person, and which may even be expected to vary from time to time within any one person, is not very controversial. It is in fact a realistic way to view violence. Ira Zepp conceded in his dialogue with Bill

Holmes (see the Epilogue to *Agape and Ahimsa*) that he was aware of having a threshold, although for him it was very high ("on a scale of 1-10, I'd be something in the area of 9+.") Gandhi had a threshold, acknowledged in his example of the mad man running amok in a community, who would have to be stopped. Walter Wink admitted to being a violent man trying to get better – that is, to raise his threshold for violence.

Nonviolence aims to raise the threshold for violence, and hopefully to raise it so high that violence never occurs. But it uses alternatives to violence, constructive problem-solving skills, and *agape*, both to raise the threshold and to fill the space then available with other alternatives and options. Nonviolence goes beyond Just War Theory by proposing that, if we practice our skills of peacemaking and creative problem-solving, we may obviate the need for violence. It suggests that it is our responsibility as human beings to make sure that the conditions justifying war are never satisfied.

Is this idealistic? In one sense, yes. But, seen as a completely different attitude, nonviolence has very practical application in everyday affairs, from the personal level to the global. Nonviolence is about moving people from a position where their attention is focused on when they might have to fight, to a position where their attention is focused on adding more peaceful problem-solving to the world, so that there are fewer things to fight about. In this book we have described many of the skills of nonviolence that sometimes operate near the threshold where violence is about to begin. But more often we have been exploring ideas about how to work preventively, further below the threshold, where "ordinary life" takes place.

Now, it is reasonable to assume that we will not always succeed in pushing the threshold of violence out of reach. Most advocates of nonviolence would accept the idea that, in extreme circumstances, force will become necessary to solve a problem. The September 11 example often cited in this regard is Flight 93, the hijacked plane that crashed in the Pennsylvania countryside. Apparently, the passengers on that plane took violent action against the hijackers, and in doing so prevented the destruction of government targets in Washington, DC. Would we have wanted those passengers, in the name of nonviolence, not to have risen up against the men who had taken control of the plane? No. In such circumstances, violent action to prevent even greater violence may be the only option available to people of good will. The problem is that people so often resort to violence while they still have other options available to them.

Advocates of nonviolence observe that Just War Theory is often used to rationalize violence. Paul Robinson's article "Willing to kill but not to die," on the NATO bombing of Kosovo, is a powerful critique of the tendency of military powers to claim that the criteria of JWT have been satisfied, when in fact they have not, or when the question is at least still debatable. The implication is disturbing: rather than guarding against violence until certain conditions are met, JWT is available to the violence-prone, and to those trying to make up their minds, as an excuse for engaging in violence.

As we have noted previously, virtually every act of violence is justified in the mind of the violent actor as some kind of self-defense or legitimate response to threat, and therefore is felt to be necessary, at least for the moment. In nonviolence education, we are sometimes asked why we do not place more emphasis on proper ways to defend oneself. We try not to over-emphasize self-defense and other justifications, because people do not lack excuses for violence; quite the contrary – this is an area where human beings are already abundantly endowed. Highlighting self-defense keeps people thinking in old defensive, adversarial, reactive ways. Nonviolence represents a new way of thinking, not only about threat, but about all the times between threats.

All of us do need alternative approaches to dealing with threat. Nonviolence offers a range of alternatives to the usual "fight or flight" dichotomy. This is not to say that nonviolence will always work as intended. But tragically, for lack of a guarantee that it will work in the face of threat, nonviolence is seldom put to the test. Also, we easily forget that violence almost never works as we imagine it will; in fact, violence should be seen as a signal of failure to solve problems successfully.

So, what are some examples of nonviolent thinking in response to threat? Here are a few suggestions out of a vast repertoire of possibilities, ranging from the commonplace to the unexpectedly creative:

Consider the portion of the truth owned by your enemy. Consider the contribution that you may be making to the problem. Ask whether you have, and want, all the facts. Make an unexpected human gesture that transforms the situation. Invite your opponent to tea. "Send in a thousand grandmothers."[54] Refuse to insult and demean. Apologize. Talk, don't run away. Clearly state what you think is just, because maybe your enemy doesn't know. Grant amnesty. Provide constructive work. Offer a better deal. Ask your enemy to decide on a fair settlement, and then accept it. Build

157

the opponent a school or hospital. Resist denial; accept that the situation is complicated and difficult. Forgive. Ask for mediation. Send a gift. Recall when you were friends, and stop calling him or her evil. Remove a threat that you hold over your enemy. Refuse to hate. Accept the decision of an arbitrator. Let it go. Go for life imprisonment rather than the death penalty. Support restorative justice over retribution. Say thank you. Regard violence as your real enemy. Be the one to stop the cycle of mutual humiliation, injury, and destruction. Find a way to be partners. Escape from the trap of enemy thinking. Consider *agape*. Consider *ahimsa*.

These options and strategies are often uncomfortable. But they often work. They have a much better track record than violence. We believe in these nonviolent options as realistic alternatives to violence. We feel that human beings too often fall into the trap of believing that the time for violence has come, when in fact there are still many practical options available for solving problems peacefully and creatively. At the same time, we do not minimize the difficulty of taking the nonviolent approach. While better outcomes are more likely with nonviolence, the resistance to reaching out in these ways to our adversaries can be paralyzing. Learning better how to overcome this paralysis is one of the major tasks ahead for nonviolence education.

On the question of whether nonviolence is sometimes necessary or inevitable, we remain open-minded. The logical necessity for violence has never been proven definitively. But examples like Flight 93 suggest that there are times, with time short and an emergency at hand, when our options are gone. We accept that those times do come, and acknowledge that they would satisfy JWT criteria. But we emphasize that such extreme cases are not good guides to action most of the time.

More work is needed to define the threshold for using force. JWT represents some of that work, and we grant that it has been well-intentioned. However, (1) JWT diverts attention and energy from adding more peace to the world; it focuses on the conditions under which we can permit ourselves to fail, rather than the activities that would enable us to succeed. Furthermore, (2) experience shows that JWT is used quite often to lower the threshold for going to war rather than to raise it; that is, it plays into our instinct to fight rather than holding us back from fighting.

The work of active nonviolence is not just to avoid violence, but to add peace – to promote work, fun, love, learning, and self-expression rather than violence. Making the world a more peaceful place is inherently worthwhile, and has the incidental side-effect of raising the threshold for violence.

Nonviolence and Law Enforcement

If acts of terrorism are crimes, then fighting them is a job for legitimate law enforcement and a properly constituted judicial system. These institutions are charged with the responsibility to use force in the defense of society when necessary. What does law enforcement look like when it is informed and motivated by nonviolence?

A friend of ours, Richard Tarlaian, is a skilled nonviolence trainer. He is also a retired senior officer of the Providence RI Police Department with a strong commitment to good community policing. It is part of a police officer's job to talk with members of the public, to confront suspicious persons, to mediate disputes, to make arrests, and so on. In practice, officers have a certain latitude in performing these duties. They can be courteous and firm in their dealings with others, or demeaning and provocative. They can exhibit respectful behavior that lays a foundation for future relationships, or they can sow seeds of continuing hostility and resentment. When dealing with someone suspected of a crime, often someone distrustful of him and disrespectful toward police in general, Richard would remind himself to ask the excellent question, "Does this situation need another jerk?" And the answer, unsurprisingly, would be "No." The question and the answer are a form of anger management. They became Rich's way of managing his own emotions and behavior in difficult, often angry, situations. In this way he could at least prevent himself from magnifying the problem at hand.

Here is another question Captain Tarlaian would ask himself: "What if I need this guy to be my ally next week?" This question is a reminder that today's adversaries may become tomorrow's partners – an evolution of events and relationships that happens all the time. In the heat of a given moment, we may lose sight of another person's capacity to help us in the future. But nonviolence provides a framework for remembering practical truths that our emotions often hide from us. Richard Tarlaian's approach to policing is both realistic and informed by nonviolence.

Here's a problem: Many people who identify themselves as peace advocates want nothing to do with the police. They identify the police as oppressors who maintain the power of the status quo. The do not subscribe to this kind of adversarial rhetoric. It is certainly true that police departments are the source of many horror stories regarding the use of violence and intimidation against less powerful people. These stories ought to be instructive examples of what to avoid. But we have seen many good police officers who, by nurturing young people toward more constructive lives, and in many other ways, contribute tangibly to addressing society's problems. We want peace advocates to be problem solvers and not blind critics of all police.

A strong reason for advocates of nonviolence to build and maintain good relations with their local police is that the police (and the military) can sometimes become allies in bringing about positive changes in society. Sharon Nepstad[55] concluded, after a review of several successful and unsuccessful attempts in different countries to stage nonviolent revolutions, that in most successful cases, the police eventually joined forces with the revolutionaries and refused to attack them. This kind of alliance is obviously more likely to occur, whether at the international or the local level, if the agents of nonviolent social change have an ongoing constructive relationship with the police than if they don't.

Consideration of policing and law enforcement invites an important question: What is the difference between force and violence? That is, are there some uses of force that lie below the threshold of violence? If so, then we want the legitimate use of force to be in a police officer's job description, but we would still want to keep "violence" out.

The difference between just force and unjust violence is illuminated by our examination of nonviolence in this book. Martin Luther King offered a simple and compelling definition of justice as that which uplifts the human personality, and of injustice as that which degrades it. With the job description of police officers, or with any other human relationship in need of definition, we can make good use of King's approach. Many effective police officers value human personality, respect their fellow citizens, and look beyond the present moment toward the needs of tomorrow when dealing with difficult characters. They are in line with King's definition of justice, and with the practical ideal of nonviolence. It is not easy, but that can also be said of nonviolence in general.

In many jurisdictions today, the professional training received by officers in police academies acknowledges the values of respect and human rights. These values also agree with and are strengthened by the personal beliefs of many individual officers. A continuing task for police training will be to present these values within a larger framework that motivates and educates all officers to perform their duties as confidently and nonviolently as possible.

As a society, we have not outgrown our need for the police. The question is what kind of policing we will demand, and support.

Nonviolence in Corrections

Prisons embody society's overriding desire to avoid the problems of crime and violence. The goal of *solving* these problems often seems secondary to this desire for avoidance. Offenders are sent away because they have literally offended us – made us angry, fearful, and vengeful. We think we will teach them a lesson. Of course, during their incarceration inmates often learn lessons that run counter to what we intended. Once they are behind bars we tend to neglect them, rather than invest in turning them around. (It must be said that many professionals in the field of corrections would have it otherwise.) In other words, we leave the imprisoned to spend their time with and be further educated by precisely the people we most fear and despise. This approach to "corrections" seems designed not to correct but to exacerbate violent criminal behavior. Society has chosen a hostile, adversarial approach which guarantees that it will continue to be plagued by violence. What could be further from the spirit of nonviolence?

To make things worse, our mandatory minimum sentences for even low-level violations of questionable laws, and the racially discriminatory application of these laws, has resulted in a rapid expansion of the U.S. prison population to between two and three million people. It is as if we were trying to turn people into criminals, rather than into fully functioning citizens.

There are many organizations working to reform society's approach to the organization of prisons, the irrational aspects of the law, and judicial philosophy in general. We cannot review all these efforts here, but we applaud them. Corrections is an important arena in which to pursue our best practices for promoting personal change. Perhaps surprisingly to some, nonviolence programs and other forms of educational programming are very welcome in many prisons, and receive a positive response from a large proportion of administrators, staff, and inmates.

Nonviolence in the Military

If we can conceive of nonviolent law enforcement and prison work, or approximations to them, what about the military? A nonviolent military at first seems to be the ultimate contradiction in terms. Yet, if we are to consider extending nonviolence into the most threatening real situations, and into the work of people charged with wielding a truly awesome potential for violence, this is exactly what we must consider.

First, it may be helpful to reconceptualize military action in terms of law enforcement rather than war. If nonviolence can influence the use of force in policing, the same principles may well carry over to national defense. One can discern moves in this direction over the past century, at least in the rhetoric used to describe and justify the use of military force. The Korean War was called a police action. The United States is said to play the role of the world's policeman. And so on. However, a serious reframing of the role of the military as enforcing the law may be helpful. For one thing, the principle of proportionality seems to be observed more carefully in the work of most law enforcement agencies than in the work of war. "Collateral damage" is not accepted and swept under the rug in police work as it often is in war. Strategies for minimizing violence and destruction are more central to policing, which takes place in the community, than in war, which if possible is carried out in the enemy's community. So, a shift away from large-scale violence toward a more measured use of force might begin with thinking of the military's job in terms of law enforcement, and imagining what that would look like.

Nonviolence has its own forms of fighting, and we have discussed many of them in this book. The activist Bernard LaFayette Jr. embraces the metaphor of nonviolent warriors, trained to fight injustice. The Montgomery bus boycott has been described as a nonviolent war, and its veterans, when they gather, have all the *esprit de corps,* and recapture all the past camaraderie, of any veterans' organization. Today there are Peace Brigade groups, which interpose themselves in zones of conflict, and there are proposals to create national or international military units to do the same. The military do not always need to go to war. They can also go to keep peace, and work to prevent war using the large repertoire of skills that nonviolence requires and teaches.

Military force is an instrument of a nation's foreign policy, and so we should also re-imagine the role of nonviolence in foreign affairs. Sadly, countries often do not practice the same values internationally that they espouse at home. A nation may stand for democracy, freedom, and self-determination, and yet its foreign policy may have the effect of denying these rights to other people through interference in elections, support for ruthless dictators, and other forms of diplomatic violence. A good start toward a nonviolent foreign policy for the United States would be to consistently promote its own ideals, rather than their opposites, overseas. Then it would be more likely that a proper role for the U.S. military in this dangerous world could be agreed upon.

Large-Scale Nonviolence in History

It may be true, as Walter Wink has said, that the world is not ready for real nonviolence. However, it must be ready for whatever it <u>is</u> ready for – that is, for the steps that can be

165

taken in this generation to move us toward nonviolence. We need to think of nonviolence in broad, relative, and practical terms if we are to take these steps, because they will not necessarily look like "pure" nonviolence.

Actually, history provides quite a few examples of large-scale nonviolence – democracy, laws, courts, human service programs, education. Over time, the impact of these forms of nonviolent problem solving has tended to increase. For example, the voting franchise in the United States has expanded steadily from a few white men, to former slaves, to women, and finally to 18-year-olds. Higher education was once the privilege of only a few, but now is the expectation of about half the population. In just the past generation, shelters for victims of domestic violence have grown and spread in the United States to provide a wonderful example of a nonviolent response to a problem of violence in society. The shelters are not places of pure pacifism; they are very hands-on, nuts-and-bolts, practical problem-solving places. But two generations ago they hardly existed.

Viewed in this way, there has been progress toward a more nonviolent world. However, the word nonviolence is usually not associated with these examples. We wonder why, and we invite you to re-examine what nonviolence really means, with these examples in mind.

In the Final Analysis

If we are successful in building a peaceful world – a good world of work and love and fun and fellowship and fulfilling self-expression – it will not feel like "violence prevention." But, incidentally, it will be so.

This feature of nonviolence, that when it is successful it makes the thought of violence recede and the word nonviolence itself seem less relevant because of its etymology, is frustratingly ironic. It is as if during every period of daylight we forgot about the phenomenon of darkness. When violence is out of sight, it is kept out of mind by powerful forces of avoidance and denial. New ways of thinking are necessary both to build a peaceful world, and to hold forgetting at bay in the process.

We have a new paradigm to teach, a third path to replace the old dichotomy of complacency and violence. This third path is, as Gandhi said, is not really so new; he said that it was as old as the hills. It only seems new each time it is rediscovered. Nonviolence continues to be reborn century after century, with new refinements and examples added each time. From the *ahimsa* of Buddha to the *agape* of Jesus, to the moral outrage of Thoreau and Tolstoy against unjust state power, to the syntheses of Mahatma Gandhi and Martin Luther King in the twentieth century, to the work of so many workers for peaceful solutions to the world's problems who were largely unknown before winning the Nobel Peace Prize, and to the daily efforts of millions who will never become famous for their efforts to sustain the world, nonviolence has grown new insights and invented new applications.

It is time to see nonviolence as a paradigm for everyday life, and not simply as a courageous and counterintuitive approach that we are driven to by new crises. Our challenge in the years ahead will be to see in nonviolence a basic ethical and practical foundation for all of life, not just for the one percent in which we feel threatened. The task of extending nonviolence into the other ninety-nine percent is a worthy one for all of us.

Part II. Agape and Ahimsa: Twin Roots of Nonviolence

Two ideas, expressed in two different languages and from two different cultural traditions, sit side by side at the core of nonviolence. They are *agape* (usually pronounced "ah gah′pay"), a Greek word meaning unconditional love or good will toward others; and *ahimsa* (pronounced "ah him′sah"), a Sanskrit word meaning non-injury. Taking a long view of history, these two ancient concepts can be viewed as the twin origins or roots of what we call nonviolence today.

Nonviolence today is emerging as an alternative not only to violence but to enemy thinking in general. Students of both Gandhi's leadership in the struggle for India's independence and Martin Luther King's leadership of the U.S. Civil Rights Movement learn quickly that nonviolent social change requires a strong commitment to both non-injury and love of others.

In what follows we will explore *agape* and *ahimsa*, and tell some stories to illustrate them, each in its own traditional context. Then we will look at how the two combine - a synthesis that is particularly visible in Gandhi's work and writing about nonviolence as a way of life, a way of relating to others, and a way of pursuing goals.

We will start with *agape*, not because of any claim that it came first historically, but because Gandhi's interest in Christian nonviolence seized on this idea from outside his own cultural tradition, and made it central to his own philosophy. *Ahimsa*, the word that does come from his own cultural tradition, may translate more directly than does *agape* into the English word nonviolence, but to most proponents, the modern meaning of nonviolence necessarily combines non-injury with love. And of the two, it is love, not just the behavioral avoidance of physical violence, that animates nonviolence and makes it a dynamic force.

Chapter 6 - Agape

Agape is an ancient Greek word, but its meaning in our modern world has been largely shaped by Christian writings, interpretations, and usage. So, we will begin by looking at biblical references to *agape*, and then move outward from there.

Agape in the Bible

Tucked away in the pre-Christian Greek language was a word for love rarely used before the Bible's New Testament. Early Christian writers, in their Gospels and Letters (primarily those of Paul and John), resurrected this heretofore obscure word, *agape*. *Agape is* almost untranslatable into English, but it was put into service to describe the extravagant, unconditional love for humanity implied by the idea of God sending Jesus as a human person into the world, to teach, to be an example, and ultimately to save humanity from itself.

To frame our discussion, let us begin with several key passages in the New Testament that specifically refer to love. Each of the following verses exemplifies a form of *agape*. And in every case, the English word "love" is a translation of *agape*. The frequent use of *agape* reflects its importance as a signal communicating identification with the early Christian community, with its moral stance, and with its understanding of God.

"I give you a new commandment, that you love one

another. Just as I have loved you, you also should love one another. By this everyone will know that you are my disciples, if you love one another."
    John 13:34

"Beloved, let us love one another, because love is from God; everyone who loves is born of God and knows God. Whoever does not love does not know God, for God is love."
    I John 4:8

"Above all, put on love which binds things together in perfect harmony."
    Colossians 3:14

"You have heard that it was said 'You shall love your neighbor and hate your enemy.' But I say to you, love your enemies and pray for those who persecute you."
    Matthew 5:43-44

"'Teacher, which is the greatest commandment in the law?' And Jesus said to him, 'You shall love the Lord your God with all your heart, with all your soul, and with all your mind. This is the greatest and first commandment. And the second is like it. You shall love your neighbor as yourself. On these two commandments hang all the laws and prophets.'"
    Matthew 22:36-40
    See also Mark 12:29-31 and Luke 10:27

Even more compelling is Paul's observation in Romans 13 that *agape* is the fulfillment of all religious law:

"The commandments ... (are) summed up in the

words 'Love your neighbor as yourself.' Love does no wrong to a neighbor; therefore love is the fulfilling of the law."
Romans 13:9-10

Finally, consider a passage from I Corinthians. This panegyric to love is unmatched in world literature. Note how love never fails; there is nothing love cannot face; love lasts forever and is the greatest of human and divine attributes:

"Though I speak with the tongues of men and of angels, and have not love, I am become as sounding brass, or a tinkling cymbal.
And though I have the gift of prophecy, and understand all mysteries, and all knowledge, and though I have all faith, so that I could remove mountains, and have not love, I am nothing.
And though I bestow all my goods to feed the poor, and though I give my body to be burned, and have not love, I gain nothing.
Love is patient and kind; love is not jealous or boastful; it is not arrogant or rude. Love does not insist on its own way; it is not irritable or resentful; it does not rejoice at wrong, but rejoices in the right. Love bears all things, believes all things, hopes all things, endures all things. Love never ends ..."
I Corinthians 13:1-8a[56]

Agape as a Commandment

The new commandment found in John 13, "that you love one another," has been called the 11th commandment. Here, and more specifically in I John 4:8, is the biblical link between ontology and ethics, between the conception of God and the direction of Christian life. As God is, so people are to be. As God does, so people are to do. It is not so much that "being" precedes "doing," as we often find in philosophy, but that they are a fortunate and well-entrenched biblical praxis - a unity of reflection and action exemplified in the life and teachings of Jesus.

The so-called "great commandment" (to love God and neighbor), found in all three of the synoptic gospels of Matthew, Mark, and Luke, reinforces this Christian praxis. To love God with every fiber of our being is the first, reflective, part of it, but the second, active, part is "like the first." We are to love our neighbor as ourselves. It is as if the two were the sides of an unstamped metallic disc, to use a Gandhian figure of speech. The two are indistinguishable; both the vertical (loving God) and horizontal (loving our neighbor) dimensions of faith equally need to be honed in our consciousness and expressed in our activity.

John, in the fourth chapter of his first letter, presses the issue. No one has seen God, he says. But if we love one another (not even if we love God!), God abides in us and we in God. In a real way, then, our love for one another brings God out of the abstract. That love is an icon of God, a sign and sacrament of God's presence. So, God is made concrete and visible by our approximations of *agape*.

It is noteworthy that in much of the New Testament, love is more often used as a verb (implying dynamism) than as a noun (implying a static state). *Agape* is something we do in thankful response to God for loving us. This is why Soren Kierkegaard said, "The Christian life is endless striving born of gratitude." And why Isaac Watts penned "Love so amazing, so divine, demands my soul, my life, my all."

The Directionality of Agape

Agape restores a person's broken, alienated estrangement from God, creating wholeness and stimulating atonement with God, self, and neighbor. This reconciling impulse is at the heart of *agape* and has inspired Christian theologians and poets to exhaust human language in describing it.

One Christian thinker who dealt most persuasively with the theological consequences of *agape* was Sweden's Anders Nygren, in his book *Agape and Eros*. It is a controversial and foundational, if not revolutionary, study of what he understands the defining motif of Christianity to be.

Nygren perceives four main features of *agape*: its indifference to value while creating value; its bestowal of worth upon us rather than exacting worth from us; its spontaneity and unmotivated impulse; and its self-initiating character. *Agape* is without qualification; that is, it is unmotivated, unconditional, undeserved, unending, and unfailing. This makes *agape* radically unique and unusual in a world usually full of qualifications and preconditions. [57]

Agape as viewed by Nygren is brought into sharper focus by the distinction he makes between it and erotic love. He suggests this comparative taxonomy: [58]

Eros is acquisitive desire and longing; *Agape* is sacrificial giving.

Eros is an upward movement; *Agape* comes down. *Eros* is man's way to God; *Agape* is God's way to man.

Eros is man's effort: it assumes that man's salvation is his work; *Agape* is God's grace: salvation is the work of Divine love.

Eros is egocentric love, a form of self-assertion of the highest, noblest, sublimest kind; *Agape* is unselfish love, it "seeks not its own," it gives itself away.

Eros seeks to gain its life, a life divine, immortalized; *Agape* lives the life of God, and therefore seeks to "lose it."

Eros is the will to get and possess, which depends on want and need; *Agape* is freedom in giving, which depends on wealth and plenty.

Eros is primarily *man's* love; God is the *object* of Eros. Even when it is attributed to God, *Eros* is patterned on human love. *Agape* is primarily *God's* love; God is *Agape*. Even when it is attributed to man, *Agape* is patterned on Divine love.

Eros is determined by the quality, the beauty and worth, of its object; it is not spontaneous but evoked, motivated. *Agape* is sovereign in relation to its object, and is directed to both the evil and the good. It is spontaneous, overflowing, unmotivated.

Eros recognizes value in its object - and loves it; *Agape* loves - and *creates value* in its object.

A further buttressing of Nygren's approach is made by his countryman Gustav Aulen, who proposed in a marvelous summary of Christian atonement theories (*Christus Victor)* that the primary and preferable Christian view of atonement is the "classical" or "dramatic" theory. This theory is an explication of a verse in Paul's Corinthian correspondence in which he describes God's purpose in the suffering of Jesus on the cross. "God was in Christ reconciling the world unto himself, not counting our sins against us, but giving the message of reconciliation to us." [59] In the person of Jesus, God, the offended and violated one, the hurt party, the one snubbed by us, takes the initiative and comes to us with an accepting and loving embrace, and in so doing absorbs and destroys all our guilt, self-pity, pride, separation, and self-elevation while not destroying the *agape* God has for us. That is the miracle and mystery of *agape*.

The cross was God's action - self-sacrificial but nonviolent toward others - against all the forces of evil and injustice - sin, death, and the devil - or any opposition to God's will and purpose. Walter Wink likes to call these forces "principalities and powers."

God's initiating movement toward humanity radically, cosmically, and forever alters the relation of people to God. Reconciliation has happened with no need to satisfy God's anger or wrath, because God instead was acting out of *agape*.

This contrasts with the so-called "objective" view of the atonement promised by Anselm a millennium ago in a little book called *Why the God-Man?* In Anselm's view, Jesus died for us and sacrificed himself on our behalf to assuage the anger, wrath, and judgment of an offended God. This has also been called the substitutionary theory - Jesus taking our place, offering himself before the Holy One (the Object) as the spotless lamb of God. It is a very popular theory, and has held a hegemonic dominance over Christianity for a thousand years. It is rooted in the Roman judicial system in the form of

177

quid pro quo - the offering of this sacrifice or expiation in return for this or that benefit, such as forgiveness of sin.

To most nonviolent Christians, this substitution view of atonement perverts the love of God revealed in the cross, which is fundamentally *agapaic*, that is, self-giving and refusing to count the cost. [60]

The significance of the distinction between the classical and substitutionary theories then, is that, in general, those who subscribe to substitution do not endorse nonviolence as a way of life.

Agape and Will

The practice of *agape* is not dependent on our capacity for affection, sentiment, or emotional depth, nor on the romantic tugs and pulls of our personal lives. This is primarily why it can be commanded, as in: You *shall* love the Lord your God ... and your neighbor as yourself. *Agape* is not an affection; it is a matter of our will. The application of *agape* in human relationships is always "in spite of," not "because of." We *will* love our neighbor; God has *willed* that we make this effort, modeling ourselves on God.

The covenant made by a husband and wife in marriage is a helpful human analogy. The clergy does not ask them if they are in love, if they like each other, how they feel about each other, or if they are romantically involved. Marriage is not based on a state of affection, but on a solid vow and covenant. The clergy asks, "*Will* you love each other ... in sickness and in health, in prosperity and adversity, for better or for worse?" That is to say, "When you can't stand each other, when you are on each other's nerves, when you don't like each other, will you still love each other?" The response by the bride and groom is "We will."

Martin Luther King Jr. counted on this understanding of *agape* to make sense of his use of nonviolence. We are not, he said, talking about love as "emotional bosh" or "merely a sentimental outpouring" but something deeper, and that depth is to be found in *agape*.

"*Agape* is more than romantic love, *agape* is more than friendship. *Agape* is understanding, creative, redemptive good will to all men. It is an overflowing love which seeks nothing in return ... So that when one rises to love on this level, he loves men not because he likes them, not because their ways appeal to him, but he loves every man because God loves him ... I'm very glad (Jesus) didn't say like your enemies, because it is pretty difficult to like some people ... but Jesus says love them, and love is greater than like." [61]

Nonviolence is not dependent on sentimental emotional attachment to your opponent. That would be a burden too heavy for even Jesus to bear (think of his action against the money changers in the Temple), much less for Albert Luthuli, Martin Niemoeller, Danilo Dolci, Cesar Chavez, or Dom Helder Camara in their valiant nonviolent lives of protest against injustice.

That *agape* can be commanded and willed allowed Martin Luther King to love white Americans. That love did not spring from his feeling for them, but from his spiritual

NONVIOLENCE: ORIGINS AND OUTCOMES

direction and the will of God. And, to the extent that some progress toward reconciliation between the races has happened, it is due in no small measure to King's fulfillment of this commandment. As he said following the bombing of his home in Montgomery, "We must love our white brothers, no matter what they do to us", with the implication that only in this way could both black and white be saved.

Forgiveness

Agape has also to do with forgiving enemies. Walter Wink, noted New Testament scholar, has said that the ultimate religious question today should no longer be (Luther's) "How can I find a gracious God?" but "How can I find God in my enemy?" [62]

Loving and forgiving enemies are at the center of *agape* as well as of God. Every Christian who adheres to nonviolence must face head-on this teaching of Jesus and, if you will pardon the expression, make her or his peace with this passage: "You have heard that it was said, 'An eye for an eye and a tooth for a tooth.' But I say to you, do not resist one who is evil. But if any one strikes you on the right cheek, turn to them the other, and if anyone would sue you and take your coat, let them have your cloak as well; if any one forces you to go a mile, go with them two miles." [63]

Wink claims that this teaching of Jesus implies three possible responses: submission, violent opposition, or a third way, which might be called nonviolent direct action. And for Wink the heart of Jesus's 'third way' is contained in the thesis statement in Matthew 5:39, "Resist not evil" (King James

Version) or "Do not resist one who is evil" (Revised Standard Version).

"Resist not evil" has been the usual translation of the term *anthistemi*. But, says Wink, Jesus would hardly have advised his audience not to resist evil! "That would have been absurd. His entire ministry is utterly at odds with such a preposterous idea." [64] Perhaps the hermeneutical stance of members of the translation team, appointed by James I, reflected the throne's desire to keep the king's subjects compliant and passive. In any case, Jesus's entire life was a refutation of passivity. He embodied the practice of active, initiating love. As we said earlier, it was never a case of either resistance or surrender, but in what way one would resist evil or in what way *agape* would be applied. Jesus was not about to be a co-conspirator in our victimization or in our becoming a doormat.

So, Wink suggests the following, more accurate translation of *antihistemi*: "Do not strike back at evil (or one who has done you evil) in kind. Do not give blow for blow. Do not retaliate against violence with violence. Do not resist an evil by letting the evil itself dictate the terms of your response." [65]

Martin Luther King profoundly understood this rendering of the text. In a sermon titled "Loving Your Enemies," surely one of the great statements of twentieth century Christian literature, King reminded us that there will be no permanent solution to the race problem until oppressed men develop the capacity to love their enemies. He goes on to say "Forgiveness does not mean ignoring what has been done or putting a false label on an evil act. It means, rather, that the evil act no longer remains as a barrier to the relationship. Forgiveness is a catalyst creating the atmosphere necessary for a fresh start and a new beginning ... Forgiveness means reconciliation, a coming together again." [66]

L. Gregory Jones supports this argument. "Christian forgiveness," he says, "is not simply a word of acquittal; nor is it something that merely refers backward. Rather, Christian forgiveness - and, more specifically, forgiven-ness - is a way of life, a fidelity to a relationship of friendship, that must be learned and relearned ... " [67]

One of the most poignant observations of the nature of *agapaic* forgiveness is from Miroslav Volf's reflection on the inter-ethnic cycles of violence in the former Yugoslavia, especially in his native Croatia, and elsewhere in the world. "Forgiveness is the boundary between exclusion and embrace. It heals the wounds that the power-acts of exclusion have inflicted and breaks down the dividing wall of hostility. Yet it leaves a distance between people, an empty space of neutrality, that allows them either to go their separate ways in what is sometimes called 'peace' or to fall into each other's arms and restore broken communion ... At the heart of the cross is Christ's stance of not letting the other remain an enemy and creating space in himself for the offender to come in." [68]

Agape has the cathartic effect of exorcizing the demons in our relationship - the enmity, the injustice, the bitterness, the grudges, the hatred, the violence. Martin Luther King knew this all too well. But for him, forgiving the white racist was not easy, not a trivial pursuit, nor a case of sloppy *agape*. It was a costly and difficult love. And as an oppressed person, he had an epistemological advantage over the racist. King knew something his opponents did not, namely, that the white racist was just as powerless and imprisoned as the black victim of segregation, if not more so, through his historic prejudice, social programming, and self-aggrandizing egoism, and could only be freed from this bondage by the victim's forgiveness.

Agape and Justice

A frequently mentioned limitation of agape is that it is applicable only in one-to-one relationships where self-sacrifice and indiscriminate benevolence are possible and appropriate. But, as the argument goes, when *agape* is applied in one-to-many relations, it is severely qualified. Some Protestant traditions have even made this distinction a dualism by calling justice "Law" and the Gospel "Love." Others have said that love can be practiced with the neighbor and justice only with a neighborhood. In this latter case one has then to deal with competing neighbor claims and, of necessity, is called upon to be prudential, calculating, pragmatic, and compromising.

The most helpful dialectician of love and justice was Reinhold Niebuhr, who was also one of the most influential theologians for Martin Luther King. That is to say, love and justice for Niebuhr can be distinguished but they are not to be separated, nor to be seen as different in kind. As Niebuhr said, "love is both the fulfillment and the negation of all the achievements of justice in history - fulfillment in that it serves to expand the *agapaic* potential of justice and negation in that it always transcends justice, to bring under judgment every realization of justice." [69]

In complex human relations of society, Niebuhr understood that the ethical goal is not love, but the achievement of justice. For love is expressed in social relationships in terms of justice. This in no way is to devalue love. Indeed, love demands justice, which is the highest approximation of love that finite human beings can realize in their social existence.

All this was not lost on King. He knew as a member of a disadvantaged group that, in his words, "the Negro needs justice, not merely love." In fact, King said, we must demand justice for Negroes. "Love that does not satisfy justice is no love at all. It is merely sentimental affection, little more than what one would have for a pet. Love at its best is justice concretized." [70] For instance, if white persons in power truly loved minorities or the dispossessed, they would be about relinquishing the privilege of their majority status and the possessions their power had helped them obtain, and work for social justice. King knew this could be accomplished most effectively by legislation informed by love. He even got more specific, and his theology is as "realistic" as Niebuhr's. To critics who sought to diminish the effects of law he said, "Morality cannot be legislated, but behavior can be regulated." And further, "It may be true that law can't make a man love me, but it can keep him from lynching me."

Nor was King held hostage to the setting of love over against power. "What is needed is a realization that power without love is reckless and abusive and that love without power is sentimental and anemic. Power at its best is love implementing the demands of justice. Justice at its best is love correcting everything which stands against love." [71]

Since, in public policy and legislation, love is tested by justice, the higher the ideal of love, the more justice we will produce. That is the practical need for *agape* and its accompanying nonviolence, the highest human ideal and divine revelation we know. That is why Reinhold Niebuhr called *agape* a "relevant ideal." It has the magnetic power to attract us to its fulfillment and at the same time provides a standard by which to judge our approximations of it.

Approximations of Agape

Agape, by its very nature, will not be perfectly expressed in human relationships. The ideal will always be approximated and, to some degree, refracted. It would be unrealistic to expect otherwise. But it is worth paying attention to examples around us which do come relatively close to *agape's* high standard and which provide models for our own striving. An *agapaic* God surely understands our inability to reach perfection.

The following illustrations were not chosen because they are loud, obvious examples of the theology we have touched upon. As is so often the case, *agape*, as well as much of God's activity, is quiet, cloaked in anonymity, and (unlike violence) the opposite of "front page news."

The Umpire and the Second Baseman

In late September 1996, The Baltimore Orioles were playing the Toronto Blue Jays in Toronto's Skydome. An incident occurred during that game that will be forever remembered, both in the annals of baseball, and in the annals of nonviolent reconciliation.

After being called out on strikes by umpire John Hirschbeck, Roberto Alomar, the Orioles' second baseman, was so incensed that he spat in the umpire's face, and later cast aspersions on the umpire's ability at home plate by charging that the death of Hirschbeck's young son was a source of unbearable stress for him. Indeed, Hirschbeck's two sons, John, the one who died, and Michael, still living, had both been afflicted from an early age with a serious degenerative disorder called adrenoleukodystrophy (ALD). Hirschbeck allegedly cussed at Alomar and threatened to kill him. For two years, the enraged official and player avoided each other's presence as much as humanly possible.

Alomar was eventually traded to the Cleveland Indians in the winter of 1999 and so would continue to be near Hirschbeck, who not only lived near Cleveland but also remained an American League umpire.

After prodding from Jack Efta, a mutual friend, and Sandy Alomar, the Cleveland catcher and Roberto's brother, the two men seemed ready for some form of reconciliation. It was Hirschbeck who took the initiative in another September game in Cleveland in 1999 to talk with Roberto. After a brief conversation, they decided to let the ugly incident rest. "If that's the worst thing Robbie ever does in his life, he'll lead a real good life. People make mistakes. You forgive, you forget, and move on," said Hirschbeck.

Alomar's response was to donate significantly to a foundation helping to find a cure for ALD. "We're not here to hold grudges, we're here to help people. Hopefully, someday a miracle will happen, and we can find a cure for John's son. That would be the happiest day of my life, because I had helped somebody." [72] [73]

The Forgotten Baptism

Several years ago, one of us (Ira) scheduled a baptism of a child whose parents were former students and whose wedding I had performed. The baptism was set for the Sunday afternoon following Thanksgiving in our College Chapel. That very afternoon I took my son back, after his Thanksgiving break, to Washington College on Maryland's eastern shore, almost two hours from our home and the College in Westminster, MD. I had missed a most important day in the lives of two young people and the fifty or more persons there in the Chapel for the baptism.

When it was determined that I was not going to be there, the somewhat anxious couple called our home and our eldest son took the message. Well, he happened to know through a college friend about another nearby minister and phoned him to see if he could come and fill in for me. He did so in graceful fashion. When I returned home and received the news, I was in shock. The *agapaic* nature of this event is that the disappointed and forgotten Cindy and Carter not only forgave me, but asked that I have the baptism of their next two children. It was one of the most profound experiences of *agape* I ever had. It was truly undeserved, unconditional, and unforgettable. I had no words to express my gratitude.

Nonviolent Love Under German Occupation

An old Huguenot community in France, Le Chambon-sur-Lignon, was spared destruction in World War II under interesting circumstances. The townspeople had committed themselves to Christian nonviolence, and though under German occupation, actively assisted many Jews in escaping to Switzerland. The town leaders and the German military played cat-and-mouse for an extended period of time; an informer apparently kept the town prepared for "surprise" inspections.

But on one occasion, the town doctor went to visit the local military commandant to plead for the release of a young townsman who had been arrested. In the course of his interview, the doctor explained the town's nonviolent approach to the war, and his people's belief that the Germans were doing hateful things, but were not inherently evil people. Unrelated to this meeting, a crime occurred that day near the military headquarters, and strict security was imposed. The doctor's driver was found to have a forbidden weapon in his car, which led to the doctor's arrest and eventual execution.

The commandant, however, had been impressed and moved by what the doctor had told him. When captured and interrogated at the end of the war, he revealed that he had refused to allow Le Chambon-sur-Lignon to be razed by the Gestapo. The doctor's account of the town's philosophy, and other behavior of the townspeople toward his soldiers, had convinced him that there was something good about Le Chambon: "I do not understand these people. But I have talked with them and I know that they do not hate us. They are not killers. They are not in the movement of violence." [74]

A Different Kind of Justice

One of us (Charlie) has a memory from growing up in Canada during the years after World War II, a memory of a fear lurking in the back of our minds then that, when the oppression of black and brown people in South Africa by the white minority finally came to an end, it would be in a bloody revolution in which the majority finally took its revenge on the minority, and in which thousands would die.

Thankfully, it didn't happen that way. After the release of Nelson Mandela from prison, South Africa held its first free elections in 1994, and the transition to a new government, with Mandela as President, was relatively peaceful.

But how could South Africa heal the horror, brutality, and agony of apartheid? In the mid-1990s, a novel experiment in public policy took place - the creation of the Truth and Reconciliation Commission (TRC), headed by Bishop Desmond Tutu. It "went beyond the limitations of secular law, exploring new potentials for forgiveness and national reconciliation - themes that are increasingly relevant internationally." [75]

In a Truth and Reconciliation process, the victims and perpetrators of past injustice come together to share their stories of the past, and admit past wrongs without fear of prosecution. Although the outcomes of the process are not completely predictable, there have been many instances of forgiveness and release from the bondage of guilt and stress experienced by individuals on both sides of the past injustice.

Here are some riveting insights about the TRC experiment, from Peter Storey's account in *The Christian Century*:

"Precedents for such an investigation - in post-war Germany or in Central and Latin America - offered more warnings than guidance. They showed that when cruelty becomes national policy, law alone is not enough. Nuremberg dispensed harsh retribution to the top echelon of Nazi butchers, but ignored their victims and allowed ordinary Germans to live in a state of denial ... "

"Rather than denying justice, the TRC process may be exploring justice in a larger, more magnanimous form - what Charles Villa-Vicencio calls *restorative justice* as opposed to *retributive justice*. Perhaps this unique exercise points beyond conventional retribution into a realm where justice and mercy coalesce and both victim and perpetrator must know pain if healing is to happen. It is an area more consistent with Calvary than the courtroom. It is the place where the guilty discover the pain of forgiveness because the innocent are willing to bear the greater pain of forgiving."

What we Canadians did not expect back in the anxious

post-WWII years was that *agape,* not hatred, would be realized in such an official way by the new regime in South Africa.

The TRC approach has so far been used in about 40 countries that have suffered human rights abuses but then transitioned away from oppressive governments toward more openness. These cases today include Canada, where a TRC process has led to recommendations for healing the wounds inflicted on aboriginal peoples by overt government policies and by habitual neglect. [76]

Moral Jui-Jitsu

Richard Gregg, who was greatly influenced by Gandhi, has outlined some of the essential psychological and moral mechanisms at work in nonviolent resistance. A chapter of his book, *The Power of Nonviolence,* is entitled "Moral Jui-Jitsu." [77]

In jui-jitsu as a martial art, the aim is to destroy the sense of balance in the opponent while retaining one's own balance. In moral jui-jitsu the opponent loses his moral balance and therefore becomes a potential convert to the position of the nonviolent resister. We are interested here in how the technique of "moral jui-jitsu" as employed by Gandhi and by King threw nations off balance: the United Kingdom during the struggle for Indian independence, and the United States during the Civil Rights Movement. How this occurs is summarized by Gregg.

First, the victim is sincerely willing to suffer and not to inflict suffering. If a blow is returned for a blow, the initial attacker is, paradoxically, reassured, and has received a kind of moral validation. The victim's scale of values then becomes an echo of the attacker's. But if the victim decides to suffer and not to react violently, "the attacker loses the moral support which the usual violent resistance of most victims would tender him. He plunges forward, as it were, into a new world of values." Second, the attacker is thrown off balance, surprised, "loses his pose, and may become confused in his thinking, and in short, is rendered incapable of action. In this new world of values, his instincts no longer tell him instantly what to do."

Something very similar to this happened in the 1963 Birmingham campaign under the leadership of Martin Luther King. A group of African-Americans wanted to have a prayer meeting near the city jail, and began to assemble there. The Commissioner of Public Safety, Bull Connor, told his officers to turn water hoses on the marchers. As King related, "What happened in the next thirty seconds was one of the most fantastic events in the Birmingham story. Bull Connor's men, their deadly hoses poised for action, stood facing the marchers. The marchers, many of them on their knees, stared back, unafraid, and unmoving. Slowly, the Negroes stood up and began to advance. Connor's men, as though hypnotized, fell back, their hoses sagging uselessly in their hands while several hundred Negroes marched past them without further interference, and held their prayer meeting as planned." [78]

Summing Up

It is difficult to capture the full meaning of *agape* briefly. However, here is a distillation derived from the selection of observations we have made to this point. *Agape* is a profound form of love that is extended toward others simply because they are fellow human beings. Not surprisingly, this love is tested most severely by oppression, injustice, and cruelty perpetrated by others. The expression of *agape* occurs at the initiation of the offended party. When the one violated, when the hurt party, takes the first step in the reconciling process, *nonviolent direct action is being employed*. This is the inherent logic of *agape;* it leads inevitably and without hesitation to nonviolence and to a more profound atonement, reconciliation, and justice, than could be achieved by a more conditional form of love, by calculated negotiation, by surrender, or by decree.

Chapter 7 - Ahimsa

"I hold that nonviolence is not merely a personal virtue. It is also a social virtue to be cultivated like the other virtues. Surely, society is largely regulated by the expression of non-violence in its mutual dealings. What I ask for is an extension of it on a larger, national and international scale. The love that Jesus taught and practiced was not a mere personal virtue, but it was essentially a social and collective virtue. Buddha taught and practiced the same thing six hundred years before Jesus."
- Mohandas K. Gandhi, *Harijan*, March 4, 1939

"Q. Does anyone know true non-violence?
A. Nobody knows it, for nobody can practice perfect non-violence ... Perfect non-violence is impossible so long as we exist physically, for we would want some space at least to occupy. Perfect non-violence, while you inhabit the body, is only a theory like Euclid's point or straight line, but we have to endeavor every moment of our lives."
- Mohandas K. Gandhi, *Harijan*, July 21, 1940

Some History

The precise origin of *ahimsa* is lost in the mist of India's early history and is only obliquely mentioned in the *Vedas*, Hinduism's oldest scriptures. The *Upanishads* are threaded with the mantra of peace, and in that scripture *ahimsa* is considered one of the priestly gifts (see especially the

194

Chandogya Upandishad). In the *Yoga Sutra* of Patanjali, *ahimsa* is viewed as one of the yogic restraints. [79] In neither text, however, is *ahimsa* systematically delineated.

Ahimsa means non-injury and refraining from violence in thought and action; it is the highest Hindu ethical virtue. *Ahimsa* was first recorded in the religions of Lord Mahavira (c.599-527 BCE) and the Buddha (c.560-480 BCE) who founded, respectively, Jainism and Buddhism, both Hindu reform movements. Concurrently, the Greek mathematician and philosopher Pythagoras (580-500 BCE) was developing a theory of nonviolence; however, nonviolence never took hold in Greek culture or religion in the same way it did in these two Indian religions.

Jainism, at its most orthodox, is a religion of world negation *par excellence*, but one in which that negation is coupled to a strong ethical bent. This purified form of Hinduism has influenced Indian thought and life out of all proportion to its size within India's population of over one billion people. (Estimates of the number of Jain adherents vary widely, from about 4 to 10 million in India, and from about 6 to 25 million worldwide.) It was a strong religious force in Mahatma Gandhi's home state of Gujurat, and his mother's Jain leanings made an indelible imprint on his life. Jainism also impressed upon Gandhi the benefits and strengths of authentic asceticism and the values of fasting and other spiritual vows, which fueled his drive for perfection.

The basis of Jain ethics is *ahimsa*, etymologically from Sanskrit roots. *Han* means to kill or to do harm, and *Him*, the desire to kill. *Ahimsa* then is the refusal to kill or to do harm.

195

At the heart of this precept is the radical commitment to refrain from harming any living being - not to kill, misuse, insult, torment, or persecute any form of created life. [80]

As one would imagine, this has profound consequences for the daily life of a devout Jain believer. During my (Ira's) Fulbright travels to India, especially in the holy city of Varanasi (formerly Benares), I saw Jain monks carrying brooms to gently sweep the path before their footsteps and wearing cloth masks over their noses and mouths so that they would not, in either case, inadvertently tramp on, swallow, or otherwise destroy insects or even smaller microorganisms. It was for this reason as well that Gandhi, for fear of walking accidentally on insects, often shuffled around his ashram floors. Furthermore, Jains would not hunt and refrained from farming because it was impossible to either plow or till the soil without harming the smallest of living creatures. So, they are vegetarians, and in some cases eat only the part of the plant that can be gleaned above the ground.

Lord Mahavira summed up the rigors of Jain discipleship in the "Five Great Vows." They were meant for monks and other ascetics, but were applicable, in varying degrees, to all Jain believers. For all the latter, non-injury is the priority of the religious life and the centerpiece of the first vow. One notices immediately how *ahimsa* and all the other vows are grounded in renunciation, or what Gandhi called "selflessness."

Summary of the Five Vows [81]

1. *I renounce all killing of living beings, whether moveable or unmovable. Nor should I myself kill living beings nor cause others to do so, nor consent to it.* This vow is first, not only chronologically, but also in terms of its significance for Jainism. Voorst reminds us that unmovable living beings are understood to be earth, water, fire, wind, grass, trees, and plants. Moveable beings include egg-bearing creatures and those that bear live offspring, as well as those generated from dirt and in fluids. We are to understand that they all desire happiness, and that by hurting these beings people do harm to their own souls, and so will repeatedly be born as one of them.

2. *I renounce all vices of lying speech arising from anger or greed or fear or mirth.* Gandhi was clear that nonviolence applied to thought, word, and deed - to our attitudes as well as our actions. For him, *ahimsa* was integrated into the totality of our being - our body, mind, and spirit; there was no compartmentalization. Gandhi summed up Jain and Buddhist teaching by saying that the ideal of *ahimsa* is diminished "by every evil thought, by undue haste, by lying, by hatred, by wishing ill to anybody." [82]

3. *I renounce all taking of anything not given, either in a village or in a town or in a wood.* Here is the religious sanction for begging, practiced by many Jain monks. There arose a symbiotic relationship between the begging monks and the lay community; the former were expected to beg and the latter were expected to give. In each case, karmic law was being fulfilled.

4. *I renounce all sexual pleasure. I shall not give way to sensuality, nor cause others to do so, nor consent to it in others.* This Jain vow is the source of Gandhi's commitment to celibacy (*Brahmacharya*) as part of his commitment to nonviolence. The energy necessary for sexual activity was to be sublimated and added to the much-needed reserve of energy for nonviolent practice.

5. *I renounce all attachments, whether to little or much, small or great, living or lifeless things.* For Gandhi, this vow was more influential than any other. He intuited the corollary Buddhist insight that the more you have, the more you are had; the more you possess, the more you are possessed. The foundation of true *ahimsa* is holding nothing of your own and being without property. "Having," a form of bondage itself, also requires extra effort for protection and security. Consequently, Gandhi would require his followers (called *satyagrahi*) to take a vow of non-possession. [83]

The Centrality of Nonviolence

Obviously, not every Jain can practice all of the vows rigorously. But most try to follow the first vow of *ahimsa* as much as they can. A twelfth century Jain poet, Hemachandra, in this hymn in praise of *ahimsa*, presents it as the ideal of human life and shows how central non-injury is to Jain devotees:

Ahimsa is like a loving mother of all beings. *Ahimsa* is like a stream of nectar in the desert of Samara. *Ahimsa* is a course of rain clouds to the forest fire of suffering. The best

198

herb of healing for the beings tormented by the disease called the perpetual returns of existence, is *ahimsa*. [84]

Buddhism, a sister religion to Jainism, has a very similar perspective on nonviolence. After a six-year quest for clarity and life's meaning, Buddha, now fairly awake, declared Four Noble Truths: all life is suffering; the cause of suffering is desire (craving); the aim of life is to overcome (successfully renounce) desire; and we renounce by following the Noble Eightfold Path. This path is a balanced, moderate form of mental and moral purification, which includes right speech, right mindfulness, right effort, right livelihood, right concentration, right vocation, right intent, and right view.

"Right effort" or "right conduct" is of particular interest to us. Five precepts help the Buddhist follow this path, of which the primary one is: Do not kill. This is not as radically applied to all living creatures as in Jainism, but it does extend beyond human life to animal life and means that Buddhists are also vegetarians. Personal prayer and meditation help Buddhists overcome hostility, resentment, and violence and produce in their lives a high level of benevolence, compassion, and nonviolence. [85]

Another influential Hindu scriptural resource for nonviolence is found in the *Bhagavad-Gita* (The Song of the God), which is section 6 of the *Mahabharata*, the longest epic poem in world literature. There is hardly a more poignant reflection on the nature of war and its consequences than is found in the *Gita*. Gandhi read the *Gita* as a young man while he was studying in London and its message had an immeasurable impact on him.

The historical basis for the story in this most loved, but relatively brief text is the rivalry between the brothers of the Pandava and Kasurava families. The leader of the Pandavas lost his chance to rule India by lots which were cast in favor of the Kasuravas. Within a few years, civil war broke out. The high god Krishna was the charioteer of Arjuna, a member of the Kshatriya caste. There is some irony in the fact that Krishna and Arjuna, along with Rama, Mahavira, and Buddha (the latter two being founders of two of the world's most peaceful religions) were all Kshatriyas, members of the warrior caste. It should be remembered, however, that Mahavira wanted to reform Hinduism's sacrificial system, which involved the killing of many animals, and that Buddha wanted to abolish its rigid caste system, which bound persons by virtue of birth to certain social classes. As a result of these reformations, the Jains eliminated the ritual sacrifice of animals in the name of *ahimsa*, and Buddhists eradicated caste, which meant that Kshatriyas were liberated to practice peace, not war. Arjuna's caste dharma, or duty, was to fight. But Arjuna, upon reflecting what this fratricidal war would mean, debated vigorously with Krishna, and wanted to forego his caste duty to fight. He concluded that this war was ill advised, dead wrong, and that he would not do battle.

But Krishna, also known for his debating skills, argued that (1) physical death cannot hurt the inner and essential soul, the Atman; and (2) at the end of the day, Arjuna, a warrior, must above all fulfill his duty. The upshot of the argument is that nonviolence seemed more suitable for the Brahman (priestly) caste than for the Kshatriyas. Arjuna finally succumbed to Krishna's wishes and followed his caste duty, much against his better judgment.

Of interest to us is how Gandhi, five thousand years later, transposed Arjuna's Kshatriyan dharma or warrior duty into a spiritual warfare and said it is our duty to resist - to fight - the power of our ego, greed, and inner violence. The battlefield is our soul, Gandhi said, not Kurukshetra (the name of the ancient battlefield in the *Gita*).

There are in the first pages of the *Gita* some stunning anti-violence messages which reinforced Gandhi's interpretation of *ahimsa*. Listen to Arjuna's pleas:

> In killing my brothers, Krishna
> I cannot see anything noble.
> I do not want this, this glory, this happiness.
> I would not kill them,
> Not for the three worlds, let alone the earth, O
> Krishna.
> I'd rather they killed me.
> What joy is there in slaying Dhritarashtra's sons?
> It is a terrible sin.
> I will not kill my kinsmen, O Madhava.
> How could happiness be mine if I murder my brothers?
> We have heard, Krishna.
> Hell awaits the families which discard dharma.
> What a terrible sin it is to kill brothers,
> And cast covetous eyes to their land.
> Let the sons of Dhritarashtra kill me.
> I will not protest.
> Better be killed than kill. [86]

Gandhi was an inevitable heir of this rich spiritual legacy - the *ahimsa* of Jainism, the compassion of the Buddha, and the non-violent reflections of Arjuna. It was in the air he breathed as a boy, in the words he heard from his mother, and later in the lives of the reformers he admired from the West - Jesus, Thoreau, Ruskin, and Tolstoy. Furthermore, Gandhi had a miraculous way of appropriating the very best from Hinduism and Christianity to support and fuel his commitment to personal purity and social justice.

Ahimsa as the Grand Law of Love

Gandhi's trust in *ahimsa* was rooted in his belief that it amounted to a law of the universe, a law that was favorable to humanity. He took the continued existence of the human race as a demonstration of this law. In his view, *ahimsa* sustains all life on earth and holds everything together.

Gandhi's evidence for this is that harmoniously working societies, whether consciously aware of it or not, are based on nonviolence. He noticed that "life persists in the midst of destruction, therefore there must be a higher law than that of destruction." [87] Gandhi insisted this law would work, just as dependably as the law of gravitation works, whether we accept it or not. "And just as a scientist will work wonders out of various applications of the Law of Nature, a man who applies the Law of Love with scientific precision can work greater wonders. For the force of nonviolence is infinitely more wonderful and subtle than the forces of nature, like, for instance, electricity. The more efficient a force is, the more silent it is. Love is the subtlest force in the world." [88]

Western readers should note that Gandhi's definition of *ahimsa* as "love" is uniquely his. None of the other classic Indian texts nor their commentators appear to call *ahimsa* "love;" it is almost always "non-injury." So, our discussion of *ahimsa* is heavily driven by Gandhi's rendering of it in his writings as a form of love.

Gandhi's conception of *ahimsa* arguably reflects a combination of Hindu with Christian conceptions of God's relationship with humanity - a combination of the unchanging and relatively impersonal Brahman with the personal and loving God of the New Testament. The result was a definition of *ahimsa* as love with inexorability. One sees Gandhi uniting these in so much of his writing. [89] He unhesitatingly, and positively, compares I Corinthians 13, Paul's famous chapter on Love, to *ahimsa*. "The true meaning of (*ahimsa*) in English is love or charity. Does not the Bible say 'Love worketh no ill to its neighbor. Believeth all things, Hopeth all things, (It) never faileth.'" [90] Gandhi used similar language. "Satyagraha is gentle, it never wounds. It must not be the result of anger or malice. It is never fussy, never impatient, never vociferous. It is the direct opposite of compulsion." [91]

The Law of Love was for Gandhi the highest good, and also the most powerful force in the world. His entire life was a living, breathing experiment to see how far a human being could go to embody nonviolence; recall that the subtitle of his *Autobiography* is "The Story of My Experiments With Truth." His practice of nonviolence was in the public laboratory for all to observe, not just in personal ritual. Probably no one before or since has been so scrupulously open in working out an ethical ideal.

The Mahatma, in this moral realm, was seeking just as much undeniable verification for his conclusions as were Francis Bacon and Isaac Newton for theirs. What Natural Law was for western philosophers from Aristotle to the Enlightenment, the Law of *Ahimsa* was for Gandhi. What the will of God is for Jews, Christians, and Muslims, *ahimsa* was for Gandhi.

The "grand" nature of this Law of Love is that we love those who do not love us. Gandhi is quick to state how this teaching is strikingly reminiscent of Jesus, who said "If you love those who love you, what reward have you. Even sinners do that." (*Matthew 5:46*). Love of the hater is the most difficult of all, as Gandhi, with King and with Jesus, acknowledged. But that is the very key to the fulfillment of *ahimsa's* potential.

In the beginning of the last decade of his life, Gandhi wrote, "I have an implicit faith - faith that today burns brighter than ever, even after half a century's experience of unbroken practice of nonviolence - that mankind can only be saved through nonviolence, which is the central teaching of the Bible as I understand the Bible." [92]

Satyagraha: Ahimsa in Practice

The term *satyagraha* originated in a contest. Wanting a positive term to replace the negative-sounding "passive resistance," Gandhi offered a prize for the best suggestion. His own cousin Maganlal Gandhi proposed the term *sadagraha*, which means firmness in a good cause. Gandhi liked this option, but modified the word to *satyagraha*, and then used it, starting in South Africa around the turn of the 20th century, and throughout the rest of his career. [93]

Let us examine the construction of Gandhi's word *satyagraha*. "*Sat*" has several overlapping meanings in Sanskrit - spirit, soul, truth, god, love - all of which could be summed up as "being." "*Graha*" also has many aspects - commitment, devotion, holding, grasping, force - all of which might be summed up as "firmness." So, *satyagraha* is being firm in the truth, holding on to truth. Gandhi liked to call it "soul force" when he discussed nonviolence. Martin Luther King Jr. used the same translation quite often in his essays and sermons.

Satyagraha can be contrasted with another term, *duragraha*, which means holding on by force, or, loosely, opposition based on enemy thinking. [94]

For Gandhi, the opposite of truth is violence, because the ultimate value (God, Brahman, Being itself) is a loving, nonviolent, peaceful, truthful reality. So, violence is incompatible with what is most important about reality. There is no support for it in the very heart of the universe or in the human heart. Gandhi captured this notion in a classic passage to a friend in 1932. "In 'God is Truth,' '*is*' certainly does not mean 'equal to' nor does it merely mean 'is truthful.' Truth is not a mere attribute of God, but He is That. He is nothing if He is not That. Truth in Sanskrit means *Sat*. *Sat* means *is*. Therefore Truth is implied in *Is*. God is, nothing else is. Therefore, the more Truthful we are, the nearer we are to God. We *are* only to the extent that we are truthful." [95]

Bondurant provides some helpful definitions for those

who wish to apply satyagraha: <u>Force</u> is power to exercise influence and to effect change. <u>Violence</u> is doing anything to intentionally injure a person or thing. *Injury* is harm done to another either psychologically or physically. *Nonviolence*, as *satyagraha*, means to effect change without injury to an adversary. [96]

Satyagraha is something done and not just said. As a practical philosopher, Gandhi was deeply committed to figuring out how to be politically effective while ethically adhering to Truth. The first vow of a *satyagrahi* (one who practices *satyagraha*) was to uphold Truth. In essence, it was a spiritual or religious profession, a precept rooted in a conception of God. [97] However, we can only approximate the Brahmanic or Godly ideal. It is humanly impossible to know the Truth absolutely. So we cannot afford the luxury of being violent or gratuitously punitive. Choosing such untruthful means will guarantee our failure.

The Apparently Negative is Actually Positive

Many commentators have focused on the negating letter "a" in *ahimsa*. That is, they have focused on the "non-" in non-injury, non-killing, and non-violence, and concluded that *ahimsa* is inherently a negative - a passive withdrawal that encompasses anything that is not overtly violent.

In choosing the word *satyagraha*, Gandhi attempted to stress that nonviolence requires adherence to positive values and active, positive choices. Consciously refraining from hurting others is a positive action. "*Ahimsa* does not simply

206

mean non-killing. *Himsa* means causing pain to or killing any life out of anger or from a selfish purpose, or with the intention of injuring it. Refraining from doing so is *ahimsa*." [98]

Moreover, Gandhi said that a*himsa* was a spirit, a way of life, the law of one's being. It was love, a love which starts with nonviolence but could never be simply negative or reactive. Personally, it means loving those who don't love you. For Gandhi the politician, it meant setting his whole being, with love, against the rigidity of the caste system and the colonial power and imperial rule of Great Britain.

Means and Ends

The relation of means to ends is at the core of Gandhi's nonviolent methodology. Gandhi's position was that the means you use will determine the end you achieve. His way of putting it was that the end pre-exists in the means.

This position stands in contrast to the famous rationalization in *realpolitik* that "the end justifies the means," and to Malcolm X's signature aphorism, "by any means necessary."

For Gandhi, means and ends are irrevocably bound together, because Truth is at issue. This idea appears repeatedly in his writing; here are a few examples:

"Fair means alone can produce fair results."
"Means and ends are convertible terms in my philosophy of life."
"They say 'means are after all only means.' I would say

'means are after all everything.'" [99]

There is no dividing wall between *ahimsa* and *satyagraha*, no separation between nonviolence (means) and truth (end). As Gandhi once said, "*Ahimsa* and truth are my two lungs. I cannot live without them." [100]

Gandhi outlined his position in more detail: "Without *ahimsa* it is not possible to seek and find truth. *Ahimsa* and truth are so intertwined that it is practically impossible to disentangle them and separate them. They are like the two sides of a coin, or rather of a smooth unstamped metallic disc. Who can say which is the obverse and which is the reverse? Nevertheless, *Ahimsa* is the means, truth is the end ... If one takes care of the means, we are bound to reach the end sooner or later. When once we have grasped this point, final victory is beyond question." [101]

There is great good sense and compelling logic in Gandhi's contention that ends are dependent on means. Wars do not create peace; choosing war is self-incriminating because it is either an admission of past failure or a revelation of fearful enemy thinking. The only value of wars is that they may result in a cessation of physical violence, and in our finite world that is no mean achievement. But wars do not create the positive nonviolence we have been discussing here. Peaceful means are the way to peaceful ends. Love is the way to love. Whatever progress toward racial integration has been made in the United States is largely due to the means employed by Martin Luther King Jr. and the Civil Rights Movement. The extent to which Anglo-Indian relations were as amicable as they were when independence finally came, can be attributed to the amicable methods used by Gandhi and the Quit India movement.

This theme, the necessary link between ends and means, is rooted in Buddhism, whose peaceful teachings Gandhi treasured. In the *Dhammapada*, Buddha says "Hatred never ceases hatred. Violence never ceases violence. This is eternal law." [102] A cursory reading of Martin Luther King will reveal how heavily he was indebted to Gandhi for his own way of understanding and expressing nonviolence.

Ahimsa and Bravery

It is a misconception that violence requires bravery but nonviolence does not. Violence often reflects blind impulse, or safe targeting from a distance, or overwhelming force, none of which require much bravery and may actually be substitutes for it. On the other hand, the best-known examples of nonviolent problem-solving illustrate both awesome courage and true creativity.

Gandhi wanted to face the issue of bravery head-on. He claimed that taking up arms is a sign of weakness, and that conflating nonviolence with cowardice was erroneous and oxymoronic. The issue was repeated often in his addresses and newspaper columns. Here are some samples:

"A man cannot practice *ahimsa* and be a coward at the same time." [103]

"Nonviolence is not a cover for cowardice, but it is also the supreme value of the brave. Exercise of nonviolence requires far greater bravery than that of swordsmanship." [104]

"My creed of nonviolence is an extremely active force. It has no room for cowardice or even weakness. There is hope for a violent man to be some day nonviolent, but there is none for a coward." [105]

One of Gandhi's most compelling observations in this regard is the following: "Wherein is courage required -- in blowing others to pieces from behind a cannon, or with a smiling face to approach a cannon to be blown to pieces? Who is the true warrior -- he who keeps death always as a bosom friend or he who controls the death of others?" [106] Gandhi's distinction is uncomplicated. There is a vast moral difference between those who are willing to inflict suffering and those who are willing to suffer. A person who is afraid of death is not equipped to resist successfully. If one does not fear death, that person is invincible and threatens any adversary.

But Gandhi was never dogmatic about this. He said on one occasion: "I would rather have India resort to arms in order to defend her honor than that she would in a cowardly manner become or remain a helpless witness to her own dishonor. But I believe that nonviolence is infinitely superior to violence, forgiveness is more manly than punishment." [107]
Gandhi never condoned cowardly flight; he preferred violence to cowardice if these were the only options available. He once said that he could no more preach nonviolence to a coward than tempt a blind man to enjoy healthy sight. A useful frame of reference to understand the logic of Gandhi's discussion of nonviolence and bravery is his distinction between the nonviolence of the strong and the nonviolence of

the weak. What gives credibility to personal convictions and integrity to the practice of nonviolence is the ability of the nonviolent person to inflict injury. The truly nonviolent person is able to strike back, but *will not* do so. That conscious exercise of restraint amplifies one's strength and demonstrates *satyagraha*. On the other hand, if a person is unable to strike because of personal or military weakness, that would not be *satyagraha*; it would be the nonviolence of the weak.

Gandhi's life and teaching reinforces the notion that it takes an immense amount of courage to be nonviolent, and a corresponding amount of cowardice to be violent.

Ahimsa and Renunciation

Ahimsa is closely related to the core values of the Jain religion -- willingness to suffer, renunciation of desire, the unity of all life forms, self-purification, self-sacrifice, utter humility, and complete transparency before God. Gandhi captured this Jain heritage in a memorable metaphor, quite typical of his often hyperbolic speech, when he said, "I want to reduce myself to zero." Selflessness for Gandhi meant complete freedom of the soul and mind as well as the body. It was axiomatic for a new *satyagrahi* that the vow of nonviolence meant as much self-purification as he or she could muster.

For Gandhi, his way of life - this fundamentally religious vision that was *ahimsa* - was impossible without the vows of fasting, nonviolence, celibacy, and truth. He saw these requirements as indispensable, and closely tied to the idea of a loving God. That is why he did not believe socialists and communists would make good *satyagrahis*. "For a

satyagrahi has no stay but God ... [A person] may be a passive resister and non-cooperator and so on, but not a *satyagrahi*."
108

Gandhi was quick to note that he did not intend to tell anyone what God to believe in, although he hoped it would be a God of truth and nonviolence. It was his experience that a *Satyagrahi* needed a Supreme Being or Power from whom to draw strength and inspiration. Gandhi fervently hoped that the practical results of such a belief in God would be to preserve a humble heart and guard against smug self-righteousness.

Central to this principle of renunciation is the place of suffering in the life of a *satyagrahi*. "Suffering is the law of human beings; war is the law of the jungle." [109] In South Africa, Gandhi learned that the Eternal Law of Suffering was not only the remedy for undoing wrong and injustice, but was also the Law of Nonviolence. "You have to be prepared to suffer cheerfully at the hands of all and sundry, and you will wish ill to no one, not even to those who may have wronged you." [110] For Gandhi, as with Christianity, authentic suffering and martyrdom were not sought to bring attention to the sufferer; that would be pathological and self-aggrandizing, if not heretical. For Gandhi and later for King, genuine suffering was always redemptive. It could make all things new. So suffering was witnessing to and a sign of a larger truth.

Gandhi invoked the example of Jesus, in particular his self-suffering and redemptive sacrifice, to underscore his undying faith in nonviolence. "Jesus lived and died in vain, if he did not teach us to regulate the whole of life by the eternal Law of Love." [111] In summary, while not sectarian, dogmatic, or narrowly theological, Gandhi viewed *ahimsa* as based on what we could call a religious foundation and a mystical vision, with attendant moral virtues, obligations, and spiritual disciplines.

Gandhi's Caveats

No one has more systematically and thoroughly investigated the source, practice, and outcome of nonviolence than Gandhi. Gandhi effectively united firm convictions about *ahimsa* with a modest attitude of scientific experimentation, expecting knowledge in this most important area to grow over time. His introduction to the *Autobiography* states it well. "Far be it from me to claim any degree of perfection for these experiments. I claim for them nothing more than does a scientist who, though he conducts his experiments with the utmost accuracy, forethought, and minuteness, never claims any finality about his conclusion, but keeps an open mind regarding them." [112]

There is no question that Gandhi felt *ahimsa* could be used most of the time and that human and divine nature were on its side. But it is significant that he saw reasonable exceptions to the general rule of *ahimsa*. We have already mentioned his acceptance of violence if cowardice was the only alternative. He dismissed as examples the "violence" of a surgeon who causes necessary pain with the patient's consent, and of one who must destroy a rabid dog who is a menace to the neighborhood, and even of the social revolutionary who commits crimes for the benefit of the greater society. [113].

Perhaps the most revealing of these exceptions comes from a chat he had with his son and the story of the wild man in a village. First the conversation with his son: "Thus when my eldest son asked me what he should have done, had he been present when I was almost fatally assaulted in 1908, whether he should have used physical force which he could and wanted to use, and defended me, I told him that it was his duty to defend me even by using violence. Hence it was that I took part in the Boer War, the so-called Zulu Rebellion, and the late war. Hence also do I advocate training in arms for those who believe in the method of violence." [114] These are hardly the words of a purist or one who seeks by fiat to universalize his version and practices of nonviolence.

Second, the reference to the wild man in a village: "Taking life may be a duty. We do destroy as much life as we think necessary for sustaining our body. Thus, for food we take life, vegetable and others, and for health we destroy mosquitoes and the like by the use of disinfectants, etc., and we do not think that we are guilty of irreligion in doing so … for the benefit of the species, we kill carnivorous beasts … Even man-slaughter may be necessary in certain cases. Suppose a man runs amuck and goes furiously about, sword in hand, and killing any one that comes in his way, and no one dares to capture him alive. Anyone who dispatches this lunatic will earn the gratitude of the community and be regarded as a benevolent man." [115]

Approximations of Ahimsa

It is important not to place *ahimsa* up on a pedestal where it is seen as unattainable, or to restrict discussion of it to classical texts and examples. In the previous chapter we gave examples of approximations to *agape* in contexts chosen for their off-the-pedestal, vernacular qualities. Here we look at some approximations of *ahimsa* chosen similarly.

Gandhi's Himalayan Miscalculation

In 1919, followers of Gandhi engaged in civil disobedience to protest harsh new laws (under what came to be called the Rowlatt Act) against opponents of the government. Protesters in Ahmedabad and elsewhere gave in to their frustrations and were guilty of violence against the police and government officials. The authorities in turn came down hard on the protesters. Gandhi quickly admitted that he had failed to impart *satyagraha* sufficiently to his followers, and suspended the protest campaign. He called his mistake "a Himalayan miscalculation." Both the nature of the mistake and the taking of responsibility for it are worth a few words.

Gandhi felt that honest admission of failure was essential for the success of nonviolence. This is in keeping with his espousal of an open, self-correcting scientific approach. Now, a Himalayan miscalculation is a very big mistake! The error Gandhi made was to launch a civil disobedience campaign without adequately preparing his followers in the discipline required for such resistance. Notably, he did not blame those who had committed violence, whom the law would regard as perpetrators. "For I have always held that it is only when one sees one's own mistakes with a convex lens, and does just the reverse in the case of others, that one is able to arrive at a just relative estimate of the two. I further believe that scrupulous and conscientious observance of this rule is necessary for one who wants to be a

Satyagrahi." [116]

For many, this mistake would not possess the grand proportions given it by Gandhi, but his conscience dictated such a confession and he further learned, as usual, from his mistake. He would never again prematurely invite people to enter civil disobedience without proper instruction and discipline.

A Model Prisoner

Gandhi often referred to jails as temples, and delighted in his many arrests. Echoing Thoreau, he held that when a society imprisons a person unjustly, the only place for a just person is in prison. The difference between prisoners who are in jail for doing right and those who are incarcerated for doing wrong, is that the latter will usually not submit willingly to the rules of the warden, and might try to escape if that were possible. For Gandhi, the *Satyagrahi* will conform willingly to jail discipline and cooperate in every way with the prison rules. "We have observed that the most distinguished among the prisoners are of greater service inside jails than outside. The coefficient of service is raised to the extent of the strictness with which jail discipline is observed. It is [in jail], therefore, that a civil resister's resistance ceases and his obedience is resumed as soon as he is under confinement. In confinement he claims no privileges because of the civility of his disobedience. Inside the jail by his exemplary conduct he reforms even the criminals surrounding him; he softens the hearts of jailors and others in authority." This behavior is related to another of Gandhi's concerns, namely that "every Englishman and English woman must feel safe, not by reason of the bayonet at their disposal, but by reason of our living creed of nonviolence." [117]

One cannot help being reminded of the friendly relationships which developed between judges and the Berrigan brothers and others, including Martin Luther King, who have been dedicated to the discipline of civil disobedience and who proudly and willingly go to jail for principled reasons.

Engaged Buddhism: Thich Nhat Hanh

Thomas Merton wrote about socially engaged Buddhism in his forward to Thich Nhat Hanh's *Vietnam: Lotus in a Sea of Fire.* [118] The Trappist monk saw the Buddhist monk's activism as a natural expression of his religious tradition. In a real way, although Merton was a cloistered Cistercian and Hanh a political activist, they were soul brothers. These Buddhists were not, Merton said, "immersed in an eternal trance." Withdrawal from a world of suffering and revolution was alien to them. We are reminded of the *bodhisattvas* who refuse the escape from cycles of birth and death, which they have earned, and which Nirvana provides, and choose to return to earth again and again until every form of life, from human to animal to every blade of grass, is saved.

An example of this search for the peaceable kingdom is Thich Nhat Hanh's defense of Buddhist monks' self-immolation during the Vietnam War. This defense was included in a letter to Martin Luther King, who was soon to nominate Thich Nhat Hanh for the Nobel Peace Prize. Nhat Hanh stressed that the Buddhist monk was not committing suicide. The aim was "at alarming, at moving the hearts of the oppressors, and at calling the attention of the world to the suffering endured then by the Vietnamese. To burn oneself by fire is to prove that what one is saying is of utmost importance ... The importance is not to take one's life, but to burn. What he really aims at is the expression of his will and determination, not death. In the Buddhist belief, life is not confined to a period of 60 or 80 or 100 years; life is eternal. Life is not confined to this body; life is universal. To express will by burning oneself, therefore, is not to commit an act of destruction but to perform an act of construction, that is, to suffer and die for the sake of one's people."

Thich Nhat Hanh saw the direct relation between religious-spiritual profession and social-conomic life on the other. He encouraged Martin Luther King by saying "You cannot be silent since you have already been in action and you are in action because, in you, God is in action, too." He concluded the letter with a prayer that one of his students had written: "Lord Buddha, help us to be alert to realize that we are not victims of each other. We are victims of our own ignorance and the ignorance of others. Help us to avoid engaging ourselves (any) more in mutual slaughter because of the will of others in power and ... predominance." [119]

The Temple Road in Vycom

This story takes place between the spring of 1924 and autumn of 1925. Untouchables were prohibited from using roadways that went past the temple in the Indian village of Vykom. This was a considerable inconvenience to them because it meant a long detour to reach the other side of the community. Gandhi was always clear about the "Truth" of a campaign and the short- and long-range goals it had in view. The "Truth" here was that every citizen had a right to access the public roads. The short-term goal was the removal of this prohibition in Vykom, and the long-term goal was the eradication of untouchability from India.

Gandhi insisted, since it was a Hindu issue, that local Hindus be active in the leadership of the campaign and that Christians not participate. This was to give integrity to the reformation of the village and not present an offense to orthodox Hindus. After instruction in *satyagraha* and prayer meetings in the ashram, untouchables joined caste Hindus in nonviolent resistance. Many were beaten, arrested, and jailed. Soon a barricade was erected on the road and the resisters took up positions opposite the police who guarded the wall each day.

When the monsoons came and flooded the road, police occupied their positions in boats. Despite the water, *Satyagrahis* refused to take advantage of this and would not enter the road even though the barrier and police were no longer in position. They wanted the village government to declare that untouchables could walk that road. This threw the adversaries off balance and the Brahmins finally succumbed with these words: "We cannot any longer resist the prayers that have been made to us, and we are ready to receive the untouchables." [120] The Vykom campaign is a typical illustration of how Gandhi dealt with Indian injustice. The more familiar (to westerners) Salt March of 1930 is a parallel example of Gandhi's approach to the international injustice of British exploitation, and his nonviolent pursuit of *Swaraj*, independence from Great Britain.

Nonviolence and Economic Justice

Gandhi had two great goals: *Swaraj*, just mentioned, and *Swadeshi*, economic self-support by Indians. He, along with other exploited people, highlighted the importance of the foundation of the human pyramid which Marx and Maslow have made popular. We need food, clothing, and shelter for basic survival. Four years before his death, Gandhi wrote about what, to a great degree, the twentieth century was about:

"Economic equality is the master key to nonviolent independence. Working for economic equality means abolishing the eternal conflict between capital and labor. It means the leveling down of the few rich in whose hands is concentrated the bulk of the nation's wealth on the one hand, and a leveling up of the semi-starved naked millions on the other. A nonviolent system of government is clearly an impossibility so long as the wide gulf between the rich and the hungry millions persists. The contrast between the palaces of New Delhi and the miserable hovels of the poor laboring class cannot last one day in a free India in which the poor will enjoy the same power as the richest in the land. A violent and bloody revolution is a certainty one day unless there is a voluntary abdication of riches and the power that riches give, and sharing them for the common good." [121]

Vinoba Bhave (1885-1982), an Indian disciple of Gandhi's and widely accepted as his spiritual successor, founded the Bhoodan (Land Gift) Movement in 1951. The theme of the movement was an intentional spiritual and socioeconomic program called Sarvodaya, meaning the uplift or welfare of all. Bhave and his followers walked from village to village and asked for real estate to be distributed to the landless poor. Although its success was only partial, the Bhoodan Movement helped more people than had any government sponsored land reform program.

Today, micro-loans represent an economic approximation to *ahimsa*. Muhammed Yunus of the Grameen Bank in Bangladesh received the Nobel Peace Prize in 2006 for launching microcredit for the "unqualified" poor, a movement that has grown rapidly over the past generation. Micro-loans to very poor entrepreneurs may be as little as $25, but have the potential to lift the material fortunes of a craftsman or merchant to a sustainable level. Like many other economic initiatives, micro-loans can also have disappointing consequences in the wrong hands. However, like many examples of nonviolence, their frequent success surprises us by showing what good is possible through trusting others.

Nonviolence in Schools

Today education for nonviolence takes the form of programs in middle and high schools that may be called by any of several names: conflict resolution, peer mediation, conflict management, or peace-building. Philip J. Harak writes about this in G. Simon Harak's *Nonviolence for the Third Millenium*. He notes that the impacts of insulting remarks on students can be brutal, and how violating the meanness of racial epithets, sexual ridicule, and taunting over lack of manhood can be for

221

the mental and physical health of students - both the recipients and the purveyors of this abuse.

Upon examination of these programs, many of the tenets espoused by Gandhi and King are seen. Furthermore, as time goes on, these programs are developing experience with the practice of nonviolence that is beginning to accumulate, and that deserves study.

The primary assumption on which nonviolence programs are based is that, contrary to many received traditional religious and secular beliefs about human beings, people are essentially peaceful, and so learning to manage conflict is part of learning how to get back to who we really are and should be. Harak invokes the "Seville Statement on Violence" in which twenty international scholars dispelled several myths about violence and human genetics, showing that humans are not genetically predisposed to violence and war. [122]

Harak proposes that conflict can be managed, if not significantly reduced, by nonviolent training in the form of mediation skills. "Mediators are taught that there are specific techniques that help create agreements between our disputants, and in every mediation. The six steps are: (1) the voluntary, agreed upon establishment of the ground rules: (2) the telling of the stories and identifying and defining the problem; (3) identifying underlying issues and feelings; (4) generating options for solutions; (5) writing out and signing the formal agreement; (6) closure, with follow-up by coordinators, and disputants' agreement to return if mediation is unsuccessful in practice." [123]

These programs work. Research shows that positive behavior in schools can be increased, and negative behavior decreased, by intentional conflict management and peer mediation programs. The programs are most effective when they are comprehensive, involving not only "targeted" students, but everyone who studies, teaches, or works in the school. [124]

Summing Up

Ahimsa was challenging before Gandhi, when it simply meant non-injury. In his hands, once it was conjoined with love, it became at once even more challenging, and more effective as an instrument for intentional change. Gandhi showed that *satyagraha*, which we can think of as *ahimsa* in action, could achieve political goals once thought impossible. He also learned the important lesson that *satyagraha* requires instruction and training, and is likely to fail unless undertaken with deliberate preparation.

We have only to open our eyes to find approximations to *ahimsa* in the modern world. In economics, education, and other domains, there are many creative practitioners who have tapped into the hidden power of nonviolent approaches. That these efforts still strike us as surprising is an indication that they are still counter-cultural, in the sense of being hard to categorize using the common languages of public discourse and private understanding. Nonviolence seems to struggle against a prevailing disregard, and disbelief in its efficacy, until it succeeds - and then its success is soon absorbed into what we take for granted. This odd dynamic is one of the facts of life for those who would practice or teach nonviolence.

Chapter 8 - Converging Traditions

Let us try to bring *agape* and *ahimsa* together, in order to consider some issues that are raised by both of these roots of nonviolence: idealism vs realism, the unity of life, whether human nature is positive or negative, and the extent to which distinguishing between *agape* and *ahimsa* is necessary or profitable.

Idealism and Realism: Wrestling with the Snake

Inevitably, people must live in their own time and in their own place, and so must experience the specific pressures and distractions of that locality and time. A principled person, and especially a principled politician, is faced with the need to grapple within these constraints while finding ways to practice values that transcend temporal and geographical boundaries.

Ideals such as *agape* and *ahimsa* are very fragile in the rough and tumble of historical and deep-seated conflicts. By virtue of any attempt to practice them, they are refracted and distorted so that any such expression emerges as an approximation to the ideal.

Gandhi tacitly admitted as much in response to a criticism leveled at him from time to time, namely, that he was more a politician than a saint. Dispensing quickly with the sainthood charge, he would suggest that while his decisions were never primarily political, his participation in politics was "because politics encircle us today like the coils of a snake from which one cannot get rid, no matter how much one tries." Gandhi decided that, on balance, it was worthwhile to "wrestle with the snake," to place the purity of religious ideals at risk, in order to achieve a measure of freedom and justice for his people.[125] Gandhi knew that wrestling with the snake automatically meant compromising in the arena of strategy and tactics, while at the same time holding tenaciously to his principles of Truth and *Ahimsa.*

None other than Reinhold Niebuhr, the "realistic" Christian theologian, whose early pacifism was nullified by the unspeakable atrocities of World War I and what he called the sentimental liberal view of evil, saw this same combination of high values and down-to-earth tactics in Martin Luther King, Jr. In a letter to one of us (Ira) on September 2, 1969, Niebuhr lauded King for his nonviolent resistance to evil as a "real contribution to our civil, moral, and political life ... my enthusiasm for Dr. King's nonviolence despite my anti-pacifism was due to my distinction between a pacifism designed to prove our purity and a pacifism designed to establish justice. I thought Dr. King leading a ten percent Negro minority was a good combination of idealism and of pragmatic realism."

King himself often complained about the "paralysis of analysis" and the quietism produced by strict adherence to ideological purity; both could stall, if not prevent, any movement to change oppressive structures. His Birmingham

Jail letter was a response to precisely this issue. King's actions during the 1963 campaign in that city were criticized by several prominent white Alabama clergy as "unwise and untimely." King's answer from jail was that the time had come to stand up against segregation. King knew that time, passively allowed to pass, is always on the side of the powerful. Although a particular time may not be totally appropriate, and not everything can be accomplished at once, and there will be rough edges to the effort, and although nonviolent aspirations are delicate and fragile, King in essence said that we ought to aim as high as we can, and not be throttled by the possibility of failure to attain perfection, nor be stymied by fear of adversaries who are both ready and waiting to question our motives and purity.

Psychologists confirm that a person's level of aspiration is a major determinant of their eventual level of achievement. So, practically speaking, the higher we aim in terms of *agape* and *ahimsa*, the greater the amount of justice we will achieve.

This is a hopeful fact, which actually validates and fleshes out the adage "Don't let the perfect become the enemy of the good." Perfection only becomes the enemy when it intimidates us and so prevents us from trying.

It is reasonable, then, to believe that if *agape* and *ahimsa* are our tools and values, attempts on our part to use them and make them real will be worthwhile, as fractured as our efforts may be.

There may be absolutes in the universe, King and Gandhi would agree. They also knew that human beings do not know absolutely, nor can we reasonably hope to achieve perfection. Nevertheless, it is important for us to strive toward perfection in our human way. In this, we are reminded of Reinhold Niebuhr's phrase "the relevance of an impossible ideal."

Presumption of the Unity of All Life

In Hinduism, *Brahman* is the creative force underlying all reality. *Atman* refers to the individual human soul. Some branches of Hinduism treat *Brahman* as the highest god, separate from humans, but others make no distinction between *Brahman* and *Atman*, seeing each person as part of God. Gandhi saw the entire creation connected by the *Brahman-Atman* unity in all things. Life was unified because of the continuity of the divinity which flowed from *Brahman* through all that exists. As rays are extensions of the sun and qualitatively the same reality as the sun, so is our relationship to God. Or, to use a Hindu metaphor that Gandhi preferred, we are to *Brahman* as drops of water are to the ocean. "We may not be God," said Gandhi, "but we are of God as a drop of water is of the ocean." [126] A drop would shrivel up if taken from the ocean, just as we would be extinguished if separated from Brahman.

So, underlying *ahimsa* is the continuity and unity of all life. "The error of one cannot but affect all and hence man cannot be wholly free from *Himsa*, from the possibility, however so slightly, of injuring each other." [127] By the same token, any good we do has a rippling effect on all reality.

Since we are linked in total kinship to what might be

called a Universal Soul, the developmental task expected of human beings is to realize as fully as possible the Atman within them, to become more fully who they are, that is, God-like. It is for this reason that Gandhi never lost faith in humanity, despite its mistakes; for him, people never lost their capacity and their latent desire to do good. And so he believed that, of course, *ahimsa* could be universalized.

Martin Luther King's *agape* was predicated on a proposition very similar to Gandhi's conviction about the interrelatedness of all life. Integral to his understanding of community, our brother- and sisterhood under God created by *agape*, was his belief in the "solidarity of the human family." [128]

King saw religious and human life not as a Robinson Crusoe adventure, nor a Lone Ranger flight of solo piety, but as necessarily a communal and interpersonal fabric of relationships. The Black church further reinforced this vision with its understanding that mutual support was a necessary survival skill, especially for oppressed people. King early learned this lesson and later preached and practiced it.

Dr. King said many times from the pulpit that "whatever affects one directly affects all indirectly," and that "the presence of injustice anywhere is a threat to justice everywhere." In his last published book, *Trumpet of Conscience,* containing his Massey Lectures delivered in November and December 1967 over the Canadian Broadcasting Company network, he gave a compelling and almost Gandhian summary of this unity theme: "It really boils down to this: that all life is interrelated. We are all caught in an inescapable network of mutuality, tied into a single garment of destiny. We are made to live together because of the interrelated structure of reality." [129] For an addendum to this passage, King characteristically invoked the words of John Donne to emphasize the impossibility of living isolated lives: "No man is an island, entire unto himself. We are all part of the continent."

A Positive View of Human Nature

Gandhi and King both believed that human nature was not depraved, nor completely separated from God, nor originally sinful. The Mahatma's understanding of and faith in *ahimsa* was based on his positive view of human nature, which in turn was founded on the Brahman-Atman unity of all things. It followed that if we truly desired it, we could practice the Law of Love, because it was in accord with our humanity. This is why Gandhi concluded that nonviolence is more natural for us than violence.

If humanity is threaded through and through with divinity, then we are basically good and can do good. This fueled Gandhi's confidence that nonviolence could be learned by everyone, not just sadhus, swamis, and monks. Nonviolence is not a cloistered virtue, but one "applicable as much in the (cloister) and legislature as in the market place." [130]

A striking example of his faith in this method is Gandhi's rather lengthy, finely nuanced response to a question about how to deal with a thief in your house. The question asked him was, "Why should we not obtain our goal, which is good, by any means possible?" Gandhi's response was, "It all depends. A response would be different if it were your father, simply an acquaintance, a stranger, an Englishman, an Indian, or whether the thief was strong or weak."

If the thief were armed, that's another story. In that case, Gandhi said, "I would simply remain quiet. If the robber persists with the neighbor or yourself, you realize he is an ignorant brother, a fellow man, and that stealing is a disease with him. So, keep your doors and windows open and keep your things most accessible to him. This will confuse the robber and throw him off balance. His mind will become agitated after learning of your broad and loving heart. He will repent, beg your pardon, return your things and refrain from stealing." [131] As "out of sync" as we are with this sort of response to violence, Gandhi really counted on this happening in the majority of cases because of his faith in people. In giving this response, he probably also hoped to provoke us to question the fear that most of us have of robbers. To say the least, it is a viewpoint that can stimulate lively debate.

The young Martin Luther King had a liberal perspective on human nature, if for no other reason than that he was a member of an oppressed group. People in bondage and without privilege cannot afford the luxury of seeing human beings as damned sinners, depraved, and incapable of virtue. They know better. Such a dismal view of human nature is too debilitating, too despairing. King's various versions of the essay "Pilgrimage to Nonviolence" reveal his devotion to liberalism, rational truth, and an appreciation of the potential for human beings to be better by their own will power.[132] King knew, with most successful leaders and revolutionaries, that social change occurs as a result of hope in human possibility, and that the achievement of justice is not motivated but hampered by despair over the limitations of one's ability.

In addition, King as an intellectual liberal owed much to his graduate training and to the sermons of such black preachers as Benjamin Mays and Vernon Johns, and to such white preachers as Harry Emerson Fosdick, Ernest Freemont Tittle, and J. Wallace Hamilton. All these men were notable pulpiteers in the mid-twentieth century and dominated the thinking of many mainstream Black and white clergy and other church leaders. [133]

Most of King's sermons in *Strength to Love* abound with these progressive references, especially the phrase "fatherhood of God and brotherhood of Man," a virtual mantra of this liberal tradition, which interestingly is also common in Masonic literature. If Jesus said, "Love your enemies," King and the other proponents of this tradition believed that Jesus was not mocking us by asking us to do the impossible, but teaching us that it is within our power to love our enemies, and that it is vitally important to do so.

To be sure, the later King was influenced by Reinhold Niebuhr's qualification of the simple love ethic of Jesus espoused by liberal theologians. Although he saw some of Niebuhr's "realistic" thought about human nature exemplified by such problems as the persistence of urban ghettos, his dialogue with Niebuhr was primarily an intellectual exercise; King never lost his faith in nonviolence and thus, in the goodness and capacity of human beings.

232

Both Gandhi and King depended on tapping the conscience of the public, made receptive by humanist and religious traditions, to respond eventually in a positive way to the persistent, well-intended dedication of nonviolent protesters. Jan Smuts of South Africa said of Gandhi's strategy there, "You have reduced me to helplessness." After Gandhi's Salt March, English police were so impressed with the courage and endurance of the *satyagrahis* that one was forced to admit, "You can't hit a bugger when he stands up to you like that," and after giving the protesters a mock salute, walked away. Also, recall how the fire hoses of Birmingham - that supposedly impenetrable bastion of southern segregation - fell limp in the presence of the sincerity and bravery of demonstrators practicing nonviolent civil disobedience.

In all fairness, these might be considered mere anecdotes, insufficient to make a strong case for nonviolence. They are rare, but what happened once can happen again. Gandhi and King would say that these nonviolent "exceptions" prove the rule of the effectiveness of nonviolence in producing genuine personal and social change. If we are now just at the beginning of a shift toward a more nonviolent paradigm, the importance of these examples of successful nonviolence is not diminished by their statistical rarity. Rather, these examples of successful nonviolence are like "existence proofs" in logic or mathematics; they establish that new ways of doing things are possible.

NONVIOLENCE: ORIGINS AND OUTCOMES

Little's Nonviolent Revolutionary Tolerance

David Little, Professor of the Practice in Religion, Ethnicity, and International Conflict at Harvard Divinity School, has written a brilliant and insightful essay entitled "Coming to Terms with Religious Militancy." The essay is essentially a typology of violence and tolerance. His major categories are: Revolutionary Intolerance (Violent), Revolutionary Tolerance (Violent), Revolutionary Tolerance (Nonviolent), Civic Intolerance, and Civic Tolerance.

Of special interest to us is his section on Revolutionary Tolerance achieved by nonviolence. Little's own words provide the most appropriate summary:

"Jesus, Gandhi, Martin Luther King Jr., and contemporaries like the Dalai Lama, the Cambodian Buddhist monk Maha Gosananda and the Mennonite peace theorist-activist John Paul Lederach are all examples of religious militants who seek a radical transformation of policies, practices, and institutions, but who do so in the spirit of nonviolence. They are militant because they envision their missions as an uncompromising battle against the forces of evil and injustice. They are nonviolent because they all believe that the ultimate enemy is violence itself, and that the way to combat it is to absorb and sublimate it, rather than to practice it. The true enemy - the threat to all that is holy and good - is the temptation to give in to violence, and that may be resisted only by practicing nonviolence. The implied commitment includes forswearing all forms of force, not just those that are extra-legal or unrestrained and indiscriminate. Any direct use

234

of force is a step toward violence. At the same time coercion, understood as the act of withholding benefits, is often acceptable ... However resolute in disapproving evil and injustice, one must always endure or bear with it, at least in the sense of our not responding with force. One may, of course, employ nonviolent means of resistance.

"Nonviolent tolerant militancy also expands our understanding of tolerance. According to the Dalai Lama, tolerance 'can be learned only from one's enemy - it cannot be learned from your guru.' Occasions of conflict may be turned to advantage by regarding them as opportunities for mastering the distress and frustration normally associated with disagreement and dispute. One learns to welcome conflict in order to strengthen self-restraint, as well as to clarify and deepen conviction." [134]

Are Agape and Ahimsa the Same?

We sometimes assume that underlying each word, such as *ahimsa* or *agape*, there must be a specific entity or quality in the real world. It follows that if there are two words, such as *ahimsa* and *agape*, there must be two actual things, and it should be possible to delineate the difference between them. This type of reasoning is called reification, and it is considered a logical fallacy, mistaking a word for what it refers to. If we attempt to place *ahimsa* and *agape* side-by-side for comparison, we must be careful to avoid this problem.

Now, lexicographers do compile dictionaries to provide the agreed-upon meanings of words as well as can be done through study, discussion, and consensus. However, individual human beings do not carry dictionary definitions around in their heads. Instead, each person operates on the basis of his or her understanding of a word - and understanding, which can grow and change over time, can be very personal.

In this short book we have encountered several attempts to distinguish between *agape* and *ahimsa*, for example, by treating one as means and the other as end. Interestingly in this regard, we have heard people arguing over which is means and which is end – a debate we regret because it misses the main point. Recognizing that means may influence ends does not really depend on taking a position in this debate. Yet many of us like to codify our understanding in simple word formulas (e.g. "*ahimsa* is the means") that unnecessarily disguise understanding, oversimplify it, and magnify contrasts with the word formulas of others while hiding deeper similarities.

We have decided not to formally define, or sharply distinguish between, *ahimsa* and *agape*, because we do not believe that precise lexical differentiation is the key need. What we most need is a synthesis, not an analysis. That is, we need to move our understanding of nonviolence toward inclusion of both *ahimsa* and *agape*, putting them together rather than drawing fine distinctions between them.

As Stephen Jay Gould said about the understanding of biological species and their differences, sometimes the best explanations are historical. Similarly, a person's understanding of a term can and should be influenced by the term's historical and cultural context.

Agape means love, but in the culture of ancient Greece there were several words for love, and the term *agape* stands in that context. To Jesus, who asked us to love one another, *agape* became the foundation for Christianity's vision of social life. When a person thinks of *agape*, these historical and cultural connotations should come to mind.

Ahimsa means non-injury, but in Hinduism as interpreted for us by Gandhi, this is more than a commandment; *ahimsa* is viewed as an inherent part of human and universal nature. From his knowledge of Christian *agape*, Gandhi grafted love onto *ahimsa*; in his world view, this was a natural marriage of concepts. He also helped coin the term *satyagraha*, to signify strength and truthfulness in putting *ahimsa* into action. When a person thinks of *ahimsa*, this lineage should come to mind.

Are Agape and Ahimsa Realizable?

A nonviolent view of life includes three perspectives, discussed briefly in this chapter, that a person might not associate immediately with the word nonviolence, or with its roots, *agape* and *ahimsa*.

First is the idea that approximations of these ideals are both acceptable, and interesting as examples and templates for study. The corollary of this idea is that giving up on nonviolence because it cannot be pure, is an unacceptable abdication.

Second is the view of the world as interconnected in a

complex way; this means that our efforts do matter and are not as isolated and inconsequential as we may think.

Third is the positive view of human nature, which gives hope and motivates us toward caring and away from violence.

All three of these ideas are supportable not only by faith but by rigorous argument and empirical evidence. They strengthen the conjecture that *agape* and *ahimsa* are realizable, and bring nonviolence down to earth where, using a metaphor from Benjamin Mays, it can walk on the ground.

Converging Traditions

It has often been said that our progress in science and technology over the past several centuries is an obvious fact of history, but that in human affairs there is nothing comparable. We disagree. The emergence of nonviolence as an intentional approach to social change is something new under the sun, and it represents a kind of progress we should celebrate and learn more about.

As the authors of this book, our common interest is in practical nonviolence. To us, *agape* and *ahimsa* are the twin roots of nonviolence as it has evolved over the past 150 years. During this time, the world has seen not only unprecedented violence, but also unprecedented nonviolent problem solving - first in India, then in the United States, the Soviet bloc countries, Chile, the Philippines, South Africa, Serbia, and the list goes on.

We suggest that this series of nonviolent revolutions

began with the convergence in Gandhi's mind of two root concepts from different traditions into a powerful new method, one that is grounded in a deep appreciation of human nature. This method was adopted and extended in America by Martin Luther King during the Civil Rights Movement. And other movements in turn were inspired, and continue to be inspired, by him.

Postscript

Charles Steele, the president of the Southern Christian Leadership Conference, told one of us (Charlie) in 2016 that he had met Mikhail Gorbachev two years before, in Berlin. Gorbachev was the last president of the Soviet Union, the former superpower that began to visibly break apart with the demolition of the Berlin Wall in 1989. The conversation between Steele and Gorbachev took place during a commemoration of the 25th anniversary of that event.

Steele asked Gorbachev whether U.S. President Ronald Reagan's 1987 demand, "Mr. Gorbachev, tear down this wall," had actually influenced the course of events during that period, as many Americans continue to believe. Gorbachev replied that Reagan's speech did not really have much impact; however, the example of Martin Luther King and the Civil Rights Movement had inspired the peoples of Eastern Europe to a long struggle for greater freedom and justice in the years preceding 1989. For Gorbachev, it was the inspiration of a nonviolent American movement for social change that eventually led to the fall of the Soviet Union, not the more visible and famous speech by President Reagan. [135] [136] [137]

Epilogue: A Dialogue on Terrorism and Nonviolence

William A. Holmes and Ira G. Zepp, Jr.
Edited by Charles E. Collyer

A third author, William A. Holmes, joins us in this Epilogue. Like Ira Zepp, Bill Holmes is a retired United Methodist minister. Bill does not identify himself as an advocate of nonviolence. However, readers will soon recognize in his thinking many of the aspects of nonviolence we have explored. Perhaps it would be fair to say that while Bill Holmes may not fit into a stereotypical conception of nonviolence advocacy, his "Niebuhrian realism" makes it possible for him to offer a critique of some principles of nonviolence, while also affirming Christian imperatives that are meant to encompass all people.

This chapter begins with a position paper, Christians and Terrorism, written by Bill Holmes following the terror attacks of September 11, 2001 in New York, Washington, and Pennsylvania. Ira Zepp, a friend of Bill's and one of this book's authors, responded to this position paper. An exchange of email letters between Bill and Ira followed, in which they attempted to define their positions with respect to each other more clearly. The resulting dialogue, not originally intended for publication, is a window through which we may see core issues of violence and nonviolence, and the borderlands between them, being explored with respect - both respect by Bill and Ira for the issues, and respect by the two men for each other.

The dialogue between Zepp and Holmes exemplifies a classic tension between nonviolence and rationalized violence - a debate that is probably more timeless and common among civilized people than that between nonviolence and violence itself. In brief, Ira Zepp is skeptical about "just war" arguments that may serve more to excuse war than hold it at bay, while Bill Holmes is more accepting of the ethical criteria for war proposed in just war theories. Playing against the timeless quality of this debate is the historical moment when the conversation happened. This dialogue took place in the weeks following the 9/11 attacks, and so is a time capsule recording a thoughtful discussion between these men at a time when their wounded country was preparing to respond.

Ira and I were grateful for Bill's generous permission to use his position paper and email correspondence in the original preparation of this book, and my gratitude to him continues with this new edition.

– CEC, 2017

Christians and Terrorism: A Position Paper

William A. Holmes
November, 2001

I admire Christian non-pacifists who can express respect for the pacifist position. Reinhold Niebuhr was such a person. For all of his rigorous critique of pacifism, Niebuhr remained an ardent defender of the pacifist contribution. In 1940, he wrote: "We who allow ourselves to become engaged in war, need the testimony of the absolutist against us, lest we accept the warfare of the world as normative, lest we become callous to the horror of war, and lest we forget the ambiguity of our own actions and motives and the risk we run of achieving no permanent good from the momentary anarchy in which we are involved." [138]

As one who has arrived at the non-pacifist position with a deep respect for Quakers, the historic peace churches, and others who conscientiously abstain from military action, I want to argue in this position paper that the Bush administration, for all its limitations, has offered an appropriate response to the terrorists' acts of September 11. I intend to state this point of view as explicitly as I can because, with only a few exceptions, most of the post-September 11 statements of the religious leaders and church bodies have avoided speaking directly to the use of military force - whether to its inappropriateness or to its justification. Such statements have rightfully condemned the terrorists' attacks as crimes against humanity. They have appropriately warned against an anti-Arab and anti-Islamic community backlash. They have properly called for prayer, Bible study, trust in God, and various non-violent strategies that make for peace and justice. But seldom have such statements taken a position, one way or the other, as to how Christians ought to view and react to the United States' resort to force. I think such a clarification is badly needed at this time, and has historical precedent.

The "just war" tradition can be traced to Augustine, who grappled in the fourth century with the undeniable fact that Christian teaching challenges any resort to violence. Augustine opposed wars of aggression and aggrandizement, but he further believed that there were times when the resort to force may be tragically necessary - never a normative good, but a tragic necessity. Through the centuries, there has emerged the concept of the "just war" as the lesser of two evils, and always defined by principles of last resort, proportionality, prudent expectation, and the immunity of noncombatants from direct attack. This has meant that on some occasions, Christians like Dietrich Bonhoeffer, with strong presumptions for peace and non-violence, have decided to "sin bravely" for the greater good.

One of the few post-September 11 statements from religious leaders which spoke clearly to the U.S. use of force was from 260 Roman Catholic bishops in this country. The document, entitled "A Pastoral Message: Living with Faith and Hope," stated "No grievance, no matter what the claim, can legitimate what happened on September 11." [139] The bishops spoke unequivocally, saying the United States "has a moral right and a grave obligation to defend the common good against mass terrorism." And then, for Catholics in uniform, there was the assurance that for them "to risk their own lives in this defense is a great service to our nation and an act of Christian virtue."

The statement is equally forthright in its call for additional humanitarian imperatives. It urges the United States to pay greater attention to "those conditions of poverty and injustice which are exploited by terrorism," and to be more generous in fighting poverty around the world. It includes an appeal for aid to avert the starvation of Afghan civilians this winter and a condemnation of the "unconscionable policies which have led to the deaths from disease and malnutrition, of hundreds of thousands of children in Iraq." The document cautions a need to guard civil liberties at home, and urges a prompt settlement to the Israeli-Palestinian conflict. It concludes affirming "principled nonviolence ... is a valid Christian response" and "military force, even when justified and carefully executed, must always be undertaken with a sense of deep regret."

Another example of public support is from a recent speech by Nelson Mandela, who, though not a religious leader *per se*, is certainly prominent for his commitment to peace and justice. Speaking to a crowd of more than 10,000 at the University of Maryland on November 14, the 83 year old Nobel Peace Prize winner called for a global and unified effort to wipe out "this scourge" of terrorism. While affirming the military initiative of the Bush administration during a meeting with the President two days earlier, Mandela used his speech at the University's fourth annual Sadat Lecture for Peace to reiterate that support. At the same time, he urged a greater fairness in U.S. policy toward Israel and Palestine, and reminded his audience that the divide between the rich and the poor continues to grow and is becoming "a fertile breeding ground for discontent and for extremism and terrorism." He also warned the West against assuming that its brand of democracy is the only answer to the problems of other countries, pointing out that there are nations with governments different from ours that offer greater service and support in meeting the basic needs of their citizens. Mandela, like the Catholic bishops, found "just cause" for the U.S. resort to force, while placing that force in a context of greater efforts on behalf of poverty and injustice.

It is not my intention to suggest some superior righteousness in the non-pacifist position. On the contrary, that position is compromised by ambiguities, complexities, and contradictions. But so is the pacifist position - especially when its commitment to non-violence gives "safe passage" to the malice and aggression of others.

For Reinhold Niebuhr, even during the time he was national chairman of the Fellowship of Reconciliation, his pacifist sympathies were practical and pragmatic. He knew pacifism could only achieve its goal when those who are resisting have a potential ally in the consciences of their opponents, as with the case of Gandhi's struggle against the British. Furthermore, he was always clear about his own complicity in sin, and that his choice of the pacifist philosophy was the lesser of two evils.

By 1932, Niebuhr had left his pacifist position,

becoming more and more alarmed by the relentless aggression of Adolf Hitler and the futility of European appeasement. Just before World War II, he was instrumental in founding the periodical "Christianity and Crisis," in order to counteract a pacifist trend in the Church. War, he believed, horrible as it may be, is preferable to surrender to a totalitarian system.

Niebuhr considered absolute pacifism to be a "very sentimentalized" form of the Christian faith, as well as a dangerous intervention in pragmatic politics. He argued that the Reformation doctrine of justification by faith does not offer a grace that lifts human beings "out of the sinful contradictions of history" and establishes them "above the sins of the world." On the contrary, it is by that grace that we are empowered to confess our sins and be forgiven, knowing that there is no way to live in history without sinning. This assumption does not excuse us from making our best effort to be ethical and moral, but it does deliver us from any pretension or illusion that we are entitled to claims of a superior righteousness. Niebuhr was as hard on non-pacifists as he was on pacifists.

My own choice of non-pacifism in the war against terrorism is a pragmatic choice, predicated on the belief that Osama bin Laden and the al Qaeda network would not likely desist in their jihad against the United States if our response to September 11 was a non-violent, non-military response. Such a conclusion finds me inextricably involved in sinful compromises, but no more so - in fact, I think even less - than were I to choose the pacifist position.

The decision to support the use of force against

terrorism is certainly no *carte blanche* endorsement of George W. Bush and all of his policies. I voted against him in the election, and I continue to question the U.S. Supreme Court's unprecedented intervention in the Florida electoral process by which he became President. I blanch every time he replicates the absolutist, holy war rhetoric of the other side, referring to the enemy as "evil," and invoking the divine stamp of exclusive approval with "God bless America." I lament his superficial understanding of what it means for America to return to normal when he counsels us to "get down to Disney World in Florida." Yet, for all my misgivings about the election, the President's use of jihad language, and the commercialization of a horrible tragedy, I am convinced that the United States has no choice but to treat the murders of thousands of civilians as an act of war. President Bush, for all his limitations, has risen to the occasion, and led the nation in a response that Christians can support as a "just war."

Furthermore, to be supportive of our nation's use of force in this instance need not imply an indifference to our flawed policies and myopic lifestyles. By now, it must be clear to the international community how quick we are to build alliances when a military action is looming, and how reluctant we are to participate in the Kyoto and ABM treaties, or to join with other nations in such efforts as banning land mines. It is as though we only round up the posse when the bad guys threaten us. Our policies toward Israel and the Palestinians have not been even handed, and have too often tilted toward a Zionist bias - causing great suffering and privation. Our lifestyle patterns of conspicuous consumption and our inordinate hogging of the world's resources continue to have devastating repercussions for that one out of every three people on this planet who does not have enough food, and the one billion who are literally starving. But the sum total of these, and other U.S. caused injustices, does not add up to a compelling justification for the September 11 attacks against this nation. They may help explain anti-American feelings, and they certainly should be the occasion for national introspection, but it is simplistic and naive to argue that on September 11 the American people "got what they deserved."

In fact, there is a psychopathology at the root of the terrorists' rage and suicidal actions. The name of that root is modernity, which is both liberating and destabilizing. Paul Hollander, professor emeritus of sociology at the University of Massachusetts, Amherst, writes:

"The problems modernity creates are not primarily those of poverty (which it more often alleviates than aggravates) but loss of meaning, the erosion of a coherent worldview and the anxieties created by personal freedom. Traditional societies, though poor, used to be capable of providing their members with a stable, religiously grounded worldview. Modernity undermines this worldview, and the sense of certainty and community associated with it. The cultural relativism and moral uncertainty that modernity unwittingly stimulates lie at the heart of the protest against globalization, the West, and the United States. In the Arab world, Israel is hated as much for being an outpost of modernity and Western values as it is for occupying lands claimed by Palestinians." [140]

Failing to understand the psychopathology behind terrorism is failing to understand the tremendous certainty and security provided by the Taliban's fundamentalist interpretation of Islam and the traumatic sense of loss when old absolutes and certainties are threatened. It is a condition similar to the experience of the white racist who finds cultural identity and financial advantage in segregation, and who is therefore threatened by integration. Or the homophobic person whose sexual identity is secured by the belief that only heterosexuality is normal and God given, and who is therefore threatened by the claim that other kinds of sexual preference could also be experienced as "given," and not necessarily as chosen. Or the macho male who is convinced that masculinity is superior to femininity, and who is threatened by women's rights, women in the workplace, and women's shelters.

It also occurs to me that sometimes persons who are most clear about the psychopathology behind these irrational prejudices, and who are vigorous advocates for racial minorities, gays and lesbians, and battered women, are unwilling to allow for a psychopathology behind acts of terrorism. Instead, they are quick to blame the United States for being the primary cause of its own misfortune.

I conclude as I began, with a sense of genuine indebtedness to those who hold the pacifist position. The white light of their absolutes shines inexorably on the gray ambiguities and inconsistencies of my non-pacifist perspective. And, although I believe that their absolutism places them beyond the historical crucible where we are meant to live, they continue to remind me of the truth of Niebuhr's paradox: human sin is "inevitable but not necessary." Or, to say it one more time: The hope for all of us, pacifist and non-pacifist alike, is in the grace of God.

From Ira Zepp, December 4, 2001

Dear Bill,

As usual, your arguments are lucid and irenic, thoughtful and honest, balanced and fair. I love you for it and respect your position. Thank you for the chance to read the paper and, particularly, the questions it raises in my mind. This is my test of a good position paper.

1. I am very conflicted, more than you may know, over my position as a non-ideological, but relatively committed pacifist. On a scale of 1-10, I'd be something in the area of 9+. The space between 9 and 10 is the non-dogmatic "Bonhoeffer" part. It is pretty difficult to be absolute when you live in contingent, relative history. Just war was formulated when sword and bow were weapons and battlefield lines were carefully drawn. But to the extent that just war theory was ever practiced, I don't see how it can be practiced in a nuclear age, much less in an age of sophisticated terrorist wars. One thing Niebuhr taught us was that in our sinful state our capacity for self-deceit is infinite and our talent to legitimize war seems to know no bounds. Consider Afghanistan. Have we duly, with properly delegated authoritative powers, declared war? Is it our last resort? Is our bombing proportionate? When, how, who decides this? What about non-combatants? Do we project a reasonable end to this war? As a Christian, I have a tough time giving a positive adjective to war. Would "more or less semi-sinful war" be better, more accurate? Compare Niebuhr's "sinful contradiction of history." Would "unjust war" be more descriptive and honest? Would

"nevertheless, in spite of every effort we've made war" work? Would "war with deep regret" (echoing the Catholic bishops' statement) sound better to God's ears? How about "unsentimental, regretful, realistic war"? How does this language sound before God? Can we ask this eschatological question?

2. I agree with much that the Catholic bishops, Mandela, and you, have said. But why do I feel uncomfortable with it? I'm sure you feel uncomfortable also. On the one hand the bishops and Mandela say we have a "moral right and grave obligation to defend the common good against mass terrorism" because of a "legitimate grievance" on 9/11. (I agree and Osama bin Laden must be brought to justice. *How* he is brought to justice, or otherwise disposed of, however, will be more important than *that* he is.) I can say that uniformed Catholics (and by implication, all Christians in the military) are doing a good thing by defending freedom against terrorists, but to call it an "act of Christian virtue" is a bit bewildering. Is this less messianic Jesus talk and more Constantinian? Is this a difference in kind or degree from what the Taliban are promised? I wish the bishops (and Mandela) would have started their paper with the disproportionate amount of resources (is it 56%?) being used by one country with (is it now 6%?) of the world's population. Much of "just war" talk, with all its current and attendant subjectivity, legitimizes war as a primary good and blinds us to our "flawed policies and myopic lifestyles." Is there some way the Christian Church could address, without a shadow of a doubt, this issue? I was asked, soon after 9/11, to be a panelist sponsored by the local Church of the Brethren. The topic was "What were the historic peace churches to do in the face of

terrorism?" I was asked to attend because I was thought to be in sympathy with nonviolence while a member of a "war" church! That made me very uncomfortable, and honestly, somewhat tongue-tied. There is a lot more to be said about this.

3. I'm not sure we can reduce terrorism to psychopathology. To some degree, it is true. Is there some self-righteousness here? Does this fly in the face of the need to understand, which you pose? I have to stop; you can see how provocative your essay is. I relish the opportunity to chat in this way and would like it even more in person.

4. I am judged by Niebuhr's critique. I am conflicted as to how *agapaic* love can be translated into *agapaic* justice and also international policy. RN doesn't finally satisfy me. Let's talk about that sometime. In correspondence with RN while I was doing my dissertation on MLK, he mentioned that King was not an absolutist in his pacifism; much less did King see himself trying to prove his purity (very important for RN), but he was very grateful for King's witness as a way of changing social injustice in the presence of a good bit of terror (he used "evil"). Admittedly, MLK and Gandhi had tappable consciences to deal with. I think the Muslim has such a conscience. By the way, I think Israel is hated also because it is an American colony and we've yet to reap that whirlwind. Gotta go, Bill. Let's continue sometime. It is a wonderful and powerful essay. Still conflicted and trying to make sense of it all.

Best, Ira

From Ira Zepp, December 5, 2001

Hi Bill,

It was getting late last night, so I decided to send off the response I was working on. More questions. These are not *pro forma*, but for a lot of reasons I'm working on these questions. A new Center for Nonviolence and Peace Education has opened here under the aegis of Common Ground, and the reaction of the faculty has been interesting, if not a bit perplexing. So the questions last night and those today are not being asked in a vacuum.

1. Should Christians ever be sanctioning war as a "lesser" evil? I can see self-interested nation states and parties doing it. Is not "just war" for the Christian really an oxymoron? If Christians fight even in a "tragically necessary" war, does that make it just, or Christian, or a virtuous act? Is it possible to clarify or clean up our language when it comes to war? Or does our sinful condition move us in the direction of self-serving?

2. As theologians/church representatives, should our first reaction be to seek rationale for national or international conflict, or should we see conflict through the eyes of Isaiah, Jeremiah, Jesus? I am grappling with that prophetic eye and trying to appropriate their judgment on biblical and contemporary Israel, on Islam, Christianity, and America, and how that relates to the God (or the devil) who acts in history. This means I need a reality check on my own biases, which people like you and other members of the Christian community can provide. I'd be happier going there first (to the

prophet tradition and Jesus - not to what can appear as a Constantinian privileged defense). Then, secondly, we can talk about the super-rich and the vast amount of poverty around (to which you are acutely sensitive), and then thirdly, attempt to justify our violent response. Does this order make any difference?

3. Regarding psychopathology and terrorism: We had a speaker at WMC (Western Maryland College, now McDaniel College, in Westminster, Maryland - CEC) a few weeks ago from U.S. counter-intelligence talking about our understanding of 9/11, and he tried to explain to us what produces contemporary terrorism. He included The Army of God, Church of the World Creator, the Aryan Nation, and other militia groups in this country (who feel our presently constituted government is illegitimate) along with Hamas, Islamic Jihad, Hezbollah, the Taliban, etc. There were three major sources of terrorism according to him:

(a) "God told me to do it." (This declared conviction is very difficult to counter.);
(b) Desperation, a feeling of nothing to lose, of having no future; and
(c) The internet, instant communication, sophisticated technology. (This is the important new variable today.)

This triage concerned the officer very much, and he warned us against labeling it "sickness." The 21st century will be a test of whether, and to what extent, we can try to understand this new "war." This new century will force us, as never before in history, to take a good look at ourselves. I cannot imagine that pain. What is/will the church do to help us with this?

4. Just yesterday I read *Time*, Dec. 10, 2001. (Note that each issue of *Time* magazine is pre-dated by several days relative to its actual release. - CEC) Lance Morrow on the last page has an essay in which he asks, "Who's more arrogant?" He discusses very eloquently the "arrogance of power" and the "arrogance of powerlessness" and in a way holds both western and Islamic feet to the fire. He suggests that the opposite of arrogance is not humility, but introspection. I recommend it to you. Morrow refers to Franklin Graham's words as "employing ayatullah vocabularies." He concludes: "The Muslim introspection must confront the failures of Islamic societies, political and economic and moral, and the evil, fascistic dreams that these societies sometimes export with vivid results. The Americans find themselves in the unaccustomed position of being the injured party. But eventually, when they have got a grip on the terrorist threat and return to calmer moments, they are going to have to give intelligent thought to turning their money and freedom to more decent, more responsible purposes. When they have put their flags away, Americans will have to ask if they want to go back to what they were on Sept. 10. They can do a lot better." I do wish I heard more of this from religious print and from Christian and Muslim pulpits. Is this too much to ask or too "unrealistic" to expect?

5. Wars, as you know, never produce peace. They produce cessation of conflict, which is, admittedly, no small matter. But to what extent is it possible for our domestic and international policy to reflect the notion that "ends are pre-existent in means" or that "means determine ends"? I'm not

asking for utopia; I'm yearning for that greater relative peace that more relatively peaceful means might produce. Maybe the best we can do is hope for a "cessation of conflict," or as you and Niebuhr might say, "the containment of evil"; but something in me resists that. King thought that *agapaic* love through justice could bring a positive state of harmony. My "ambiguities, complexities, and contradictions" as a virtual pacifist are clearly before me and I do not expect to get "out of the sinful contradictions of history," but at the end of the day, I lean more toward Gandhi, MLK, and others who had a more positive view of human nature than Niebuhr. *The 3000 civilians and other casualties of 9/11 have been very much in my mind's eye as I wrote last night and today, and I pray for them and their families, for this country and for our church.*

Thank you Bill for reading this. It allowed me to clarify some thoughts for myself. Further clarity would come if you responded in a critical fashion and I would be indebted to you.

Grace upon grace!
Ira

From Bill Holmes, December 12, 2001

Dear friend Ira,

If you had only agreed or disagreed with me! Instead, you paid me the supreme compliment of taking my paper so seriously as to raise critical questions, which cause me to admit to the tentativeness of some of my own conclusions.

For instance, while I agree with you that there can never be a justification for nuclear war (I could never find a justification for the Vietnam or Gulf wars either), when I apply "just war" principles to our military response to 9/11, my paper jumps quickly to the conclusion that the principles for that war have been met, and then moves on. But you rightfully challenge that conclusion as a premise for the rest of my argument.

I have to admit that I'm not nearly as convinced as I would like to be that our resort to the use of force in that war is a last resort, or that our bombing is proportionate. And the one that bothers me the most is what we're doing to noncombatants. Even though I trust the claims that we are attempting to bomb only military targets, and that we are making genuine efforts at humanitarian relief, and that we are liberating a whole country (especially its women) from a repressive regime, I'm still haunted by our "collateral damage" - especially when we mistakenly bomb a Red Cross installation twice, and hear reliable reports of hundreds of innocent casualties.

While admitting to these contradictions, and persisting in holding the non-pacifist position, I'm certain I cannot be excused from agonizing over the horrific consequences of my choice. That's why I've placed a picture from last Wednesday's Washington Post under the glass on my desk top. It's a picture of Noor Mohamed, age 10 (about the age of several of my grandchildren), who has lost both arms and is blind in both eyes as a result of a U.S. bombing raid on his village.

Although I believe the terrorists themselves have some

secondary responsibility for this and other atrocities, I can find no way to exonerate my own primary complicity in this abhorrent action. I know that if I'm going to claim the "realistic" point of view as a non-pacifist, I'm going to have to live with Noor Mohamed. He is only one of many. You mentioned at the beginning of your first email that you were "very conflicted" over your position as a "non-ideological, but relatively committed pacifist." Count me similarly inclined in my "Niebuhrian realism."

I also share your reservation about the Catholic bishops' assurance to uniformed Catholics. To say that such soldiers are participating in an "act of Christian virtue" is one whale of a stretch, and not one that I could make either. I'm afraid the good bishops got carried away with their own rhetoric. At the same time, as I will argue a little later, I believe there are certain wars where legitimate goals and consequences are met, and where it is therefore appropriate to speak of a soldier's "Christian duty" - with all its ambiguities.

Your second email poses some tough questions. My attempted answers are more characterized by hesitancy than by certainty, but here goes:

1. Should Christians be at all sanctioning of war as a lesser evil? I believe the decision-making process is always a matter of choosing between multiple goods and multiple evils. In choosing a greater good, lesser goods are neglected; in choosing a lesser evil, greater evils are avoided. Since saying yes to one option usually means saying no to other options, it is humanly impossible to fulfill all goods or to avoid all evils. Thus we can say with Paul, "The good that I would do I do

not, and the evil I would not do, I do." I think this is not only a statement about Paul's condition as a sinner who sometimes chooses evil, but also a statement about him as a creature who, for all of his good intentions, cannot avoid participating in evil.

2. Regarding us as theologians/church representatives: This question seems to assume that seeing a historical event through the eyes of the prophetic tradition and Jesus means avoiding ambiguity, relativity, and lesser evils. I think that's idealistic and a-historical. I'm for turning to the prophets and Jesus first, just as long as we remember that even the birth of Jesus was the occasion for the "slaughter of the innocents." (This is probably not a good illustration of my point, since Jesus had no say in the matter, but it's a dramatic example of historic irony and the contradictory consequences of some historic events.)

3. Regarding psychopathology and terrorism: I'm a little puzzled by the speaker from the counter-intelligence agency. How can he give the mindset, "God told me to do it" as one of the major sources of terrorism, and then warn against labeling terrorism as a sickness? I understand a psychopathology as a way of relating to reality through an illusion, a radically alien or unrealistic way of interpreting an event, usually accompanied by utter certainty. The more insecure a person is, the more that person is inclined to seek solace in illusions; and "God told me to do it" is a prime example of countering insecurity with a cosmic assurance. While I don't use the word sickness in my paper, I can't help but think there is some kind of psychopathology at work in the suicidal actions of terrorists - resulting in the deaths of

thousands - who claim the approval of Allah.

4. I appreciated Lance Morrow's suggestion that the opposite of arrogance is not humility but introspection, and that both Muslims and Christian Americans have a lot to think about as a result of 9/11. I join you in the wish that we heard more of this from religious print and from Christian and Muslim pulpits. To that end, it was encouraging to read yesterday editor John M. Buchanan's opening editorial in a recent issue of *The Christian Century*. It's entitled "Oil Dependents," and the gist is that we are willing to give our blood, just as long as we don't have to give up our profligate use of oil. [141]

5. I find quite provocative your statement that "means determine ends." I can't deny that in most instances it's true. It is certainly the ultimate irony and futility of most wars. However, I have a hard time seeing it as necessarily true when force is used defensively and not aggressively. At an individual level, I don't see violence as more than a "transient end" in Bonhoeffer's decision to participate in the plot to assassinate Hitler. Surely peace and the relief of suffering would have been the more lasting ends of his use of force if the plot had succeeded. Similarly with the passengers who rushed the terrorists in the cockpit on the 9/11 flight that crashed in Pennsylvania. The end result of their use of force could have been lifesaving. To the extent that they altered the flight from striking DC, their act was valorous and heroic. At the level of the state, the best example is World War II. For all its tragedy and inhumanity at the time, the ultimate consequences of the conflict were humane and laudatory. (I exclude the dropping of the atomic bombs, for which I think there was insufficient

justification.) In the end, through the Marshall Plan and other efforts, the U.S. helped former enemies to recover and rebuild. I'm just not sure that ends are always pre-existent in means.

Also, while I hold Dr. King in the highest regard, I'm not as sure as he was that *agapaic* love through justice can always bring a positive state of harmony. The moment that love gets translated into justice, it takes on the characteristics of human finiteness: unevenness, relativity, and sometimes requiring the use of force. The "positive state of harmony" that it produces is partial, at best, and easily corrupted. I see Dr. King's statement as pertaining more to an end-of-time moment than a moment in historical time.

I know all this sounds terribly pessimistic and close to being hopeless. It seems to imply a kind of resignation that would settle easily for the status quo. One wonders where the motivation is to assume the prophet's mantle and cry "Thus sayeth the Lord." However, I am arguing that the Christian's primary motivation is not in the nurture of some idealism, but in a saving event of *agape* love. Our attempt to love as we've been loved is perpetually renewed in God's gift of grace, even though our efforts at justice continue to be flawed and accompanied by unintended consequences. This is both the irony and dignity of human history. We are Sisyphus, whose destiny is to roll a boulder to a summit only to watch it roll back down of its own weight. This need not be a cynical or pessimistic view of the human condition. Albert Camus argued that Sisyphus was neither hopeless nor dejected as he rolled his stone along. He understood the necessity and dignity of the struggle itself, even with its setbacks.

Ira, dear friend, forgive this lapse into homiletical flourish at the end. This response has turned out to be much too long and wordy. I have never been more honored than by the critical questions you raise about my paper. They have not only caused me to clarify my own position, but also to rethink some of my unexamined premises. I need you to keep me digging deeper, and to hold me accountable at every turn. As you know, such friendships are rare, and of inestimable value.

Grace upon grace to us both.
Bill

From Ira Zepp, December 12, 2001

Dear Bill,

Thanks so very much for your response. I can't tell you how grateful I am. I learned much more than you in the exchange; you have invited me to widen my King/Gandhi blinders. And you have learned your Reinhold Niebuhr lessons extremely well! That is at the bottom of a difference between us; of the two brothers, I'm more a Richard Niebuhr person. Reinhold's critique, like the Marxist critique, is indispensable as a critique, but it is difficult to use as a platform from which to act or to plan the future. About which more later. I'm really looking for an alternative vocabulary to talk about war - beyond "just war" theory and even King and Gandhi - which might lead to an alternative way of acting, of responding to violence. I hope it is not down the primrose path. (And as you've heard me say a few times, I'm looking for a re-freshing, re-newing, alternative spiritual language beyond my mixture of liberal/neo-orthodox/evangelical traditions. That's why I'm looking more closely at the mystics of all traditions. I'm really too old to be looking for alternatives, but that's where I am. I'd like to go through your responses in the order you list them.

1. I agree with you that decisions are incisions; they cut off other options, as you clearly state. Pacifists are not exempt from participating in evil; their decisions are not antiseptic, by any means, but while accepting the dialectical relation of good and evil and in the face of unclean choices, pacifists do their darndest to seek the greatest good and the least evil. And I'm sure you do as well. I'm sure you've seen the series of short articles in the *Century*, Nov. 14, 2001. I see some similarities between your position and J. B. Elshtain's. The article toward which I leaned the most was Stasson's "Just Peacemaking" and the illustration of Eisenhower toward the end of his article, although I was not altogether happy with it either.

2. I don't want to put "historic irony" and "contradictory consequences" after the "but." I'd like the latter to come before the "but" and be qualified by the prophets and Jesus. This suggests an exegetical and homiletical issue. Given the unavoidable ambiguity, relativity and lesser evils of life, should Amos have said, "Let as much unambiguous justice as possible roll down like waters and relative righteousness flow like an ever flowing stream?" or "Hear the word of the Lord, which you are not expected to practice perfectly?" Or, notwithstanding the Jesus Seminar, [142] Jesus saying, "Deny yourself as much as the contradictions of history allow you," or we preachers calling our people to be disciples-but-with-the-limitations-you-face? Work with me,

Bill. I want to stay here awhile. I was wired by that old MYF
[143] slogan, "Christ Above All," and that the earliest Christian
confession was not "Jesus, Soter" (Savior), but "Jesus, Kurios"
(Lord). Talk about incision! You see, I'd rather proclaim the
agapaic ideal, as fragile as it is in practice, and know that the
inevitable fracturing of that ideal will find me adopting to
some degree a realistic position than start with "realism" and
know that its practice is also fractured and I end up with a
lower standard of *agapaic* justice. I've taught King and Gandhi
for the last 30 years and have been greatly influenced by, to
me, their well-argued positions. Gandhi, in commenting on
the Sermon on the Mount, which profoundly appealed to him,
once said (I think to C. F. Andrews in South Africa) that Jesus,
being the Son of God and presumably knowing human nature,
would not mock us by giving us those hard sayings about
turning the other cheek, etc., if we had not the capacity to
practice them. I guess I'd rather start with the ideals of Jesus,
Gandhi, and King and end with Niebuhr, than start with
"realism" and work in the ideals when I can. The priestly
calibration of the prophetic ideal will produce a more just
society depending on the elevation of that ideal. In other
words, the higher the bar of love, the more justice we will
realize. For example, Jesus's critique of *lex talionis*, "eye for an
eye," seems to preclude any attempt at revenge or retaliation.
We now have values superior to the latter. Gandhi and King,
as I intimated earlier (and again with personal and national
consciences that could be appealed to), took that method and
turned whole societies in a new direction and concretely
achieved measurable forms of justice. Judaism and Islam,
rooted in and held captive by the ethos of *lex talionis*, are
destroying each other in the Middle East. I suppose nation
states, including the U.S., must act this way. Would there be

more violence if a new Gandhi appeared on either side? I sometimes think retaliatory ethics is as much desert testosterone as something based on political theory. Niebuhr may be right in saying that societies and nations can't help wearing hubris on their sleeves. Parenthetically, I've been doing talks on Islam and Christianity almost every weekend these days and have tentatively concluded that a basic difference among the Abrahamic traditions is that Judaism and Islam spend a great deal of time studying and making sure the Law, whether Torah or Shariah, is learned and practiced. Christianity seems to express a different emphasis, with Love as its centerpiece. But in all fairness, in Judaism and Islam, love and mercy are in the Law (Psalms 1 and Sura 2:171), and in Christianity law is found in love and grace (Romans 12). To me, that is a significant difference, and one I want to continue working on.

3. I totally (if that is Niebuhrianly possible) agree with your reflection here. You're right on with the pathology bit. I misrepresented the counter-intelligence guy. He was as hard on the "God told me" as you are. The *method* used by the terrorists is sick, but the *message* of the terrorists and many Islamists about the West is not sick.

4. Yes!

5. Regarding means and ends: The linkage between them was used precisely and defensively by King and Gandhi. Their understanding of *agape* and *ahimsa* convinced them that loving and just means are more likely to produce loving and just ends, whereas war is less likely to produce peace, and violence is not at all likely to produce nonviolence. Could

Niebuhr say "the *more* loving your means, the *more* loving your ends will be"? To the extent that we are closer to racial integration today in the U.S. and that there are more humane relations among the races, it is due, I feel, to the way King went about his reconciling. I'm glad you said the "best" example was WWII because the saturation bombing of Dresden and the A-bomb were far from appropriate means. I'd like to hear more from you on this. To me it is a fundamental issue. As you intimate, however, it may be more true in theory than in practice.

Some additional thoughts:

1. I wonder how Sisyphus would have dealt with the stone if he felt embraced by grace.

2. Reinhold's theology is based on a graver view of human nature than I am, at this juncture, able to adopt. I appreciate the historical conditions of the early 20th century, which helped him formulate his view. The Catholic tradition, along with the Jewish, Islamic, and some small Protestant sects (those aberrant peace churches!) does not hold to such a negative, often debilitating view of human nature. Pacifists think of a relatively better human. In the small town of Darlington, Maryland, where I lived for the first 12 years of my life, there were two Quaker meetings and we knew those families well; they were a people apart. They always seemed to see war as a failure or sign of weakness.

3. But I hope I'm not turning into Reinhold's *bête noire* - that is, a liberal Protestant who thinks perfection is possible in this world and who adheres to some form of love monism of

Jesus. I just believe that justice can not only be partially achieved in history, but more completely realized than we often believe. I can wait to the end time for its final completion.

4. I think we can fudge on too much grace and on too much realism. Adherents to both extremes are often too dismissive of the other's contribution to the path of peace.

5. Let's not glory, and you so gracefully do not, in historic contradictions, inevitable ambiguities, etc. I'd like to be in the business of doing all I can, with all the will-power, grace, and dedication I have, to resolve them this side of heaven. Is that what discipleship is about? Thanks so much again, Bill. You've allowed me the chance to exchange, at a pretty deep level, some important issues, and your response has been very helpful for romantic Ira. I'd give you a big hug if you were here.

Ira

From Bill Holmes, December 18, 2001

Dear Ira,

The Trollinger article in the latest *Christian Century* was provocative and well balanced. [144] It gave a helpful overview of shades of difference in the historic peace churches, as well as lifting up some voices of dissent to a pacifist response to 9/11.

As you would expect, I resonated most with Quakers Scott Simon and David Johns. It seems to me that these two men retain their pragmatic pacifism while seriously asking, "What nonviolent options did we have to the 9/11 attacks?" Simon concludes, "...the U.S. has no sane alternative but to wage war, and wage it with unflinching resolution." Johns concludes, "The current military campaign may not be perfect," but is something "we need to do" as one component of response to the threat of future terrorist attacks.

The quotation I had some questions about was from J. Denny Weaver, who contends, "It is unfair to assume that pacifists, who did not create the situation in the first place ... can now be parachuted into the middle of the [crisis] with a ready-made solution." In fairness to Professor Weaver, it is likely that he has indicated in other writings what specific changes in U.S. foreign policy would likely have prevented 9/11. Otherwise, he would be in danger of assuming a dilettante position, and speaking to history from outside of history.

While Professor James Juhnke raises the same objection to folks who have "applied principles of violence and force that have not worked" but now demand solutions from the pacifists, he is able to match his objection with a concrete alternative - an international police force to bring terrorists to justice before an international court. While resorting to "the least force necessary," he is at least willing to be specific in offering a different strategy. Now, the only question is, "How much force would be necessary to succeed?" This is a question over which non-utopian pacifists might well disagree, but in any instance, the need for force would be acknowledged. Or, as David Johns confesses, he cannot understand "what unilateral nonviolence would look like as American foreign policy."

Anyhow, the article certainly adds to our dialogue, and I appreciate your pointing it out to me.

Warmest regards,
Bill

From Ira Zepp, January 5, 2002

Hi Bill,

Thank you for your piece in *The Connection.* [145] Only you could articulate that position with such clarity and grace. I'm sure it will be well received and very helpful to many of us. It surely has been for me. I'm still concerned about a few things.

1. I mentioned earlier my misgivings concerning Niebuhr's assumptions about and understanding of human nature and history. I am haunted by his "simple Jesus love monism," and how difficult it is to translate that into public and international policy. What does discipleship and its cost mean here?

2. There is a Constantinian tinge about the piece which also bothers me. My understanding of the first couple of centuries of Christianity is that they were a (pretty effective) underground resistance movement and that being a soldier was virtually unheard of for those early generations. When

Constantine gave the Church political sanction and we got in bed with the empire, it became necessary for Augustine to come up with the just war theory - the work of Natural Law. Otherwise, we might have all ended up as Mennonites, and other "peace-church-ites."

3. It is painful to say this, but I have heard many preachers, including myself, who believe God acts in history, fulminate against godless nations and how God judges the latter through acts of history. I've even used "O Assyria, the rod of my anger and staff of my fury, against a godless (God bless Israel) nation I send you." [146] But usually at a safe distance. What is God saying to us through 9/11? How does Niebuhr help us here? Was he not an advisor to several presidents after 1932's "Moral Man" and his realism? [147] Should we Christians ever give power a pass? Bill, I've benefited greatly from your stimulating thoughts and the entire conversation. Thanks again. I'm looking forward to seeing you later in the month at our meeting. Have a great 2002.

Ira.

From Ira Zepp, January 16, 2002

Hi Bill,

I'm sure you saw the piece in the *Century* yesterday entitled "Caught in the Middle," by Michael Macdonald. [148] It reflects several themes in our conversation and I find intriguing his "plague on both if not more of your houses." I like it because he raises more questions than answers. My question from reading him is "When do the "truisms" or the "sloganeering," e.g. "violence in all of its forms and expressions is contrary to God's purpose for the world" and "love is stronger than all the forces of evil" cease being "truisms" and "slogans" and/or how do we go about implementing them and have them be more visible as options for national and international policy? How best can we apply (admittedly a refraction of) Jesus in social and political life with as much of his ideals in place as possible? As I understand your concern, it is not an either/or position, but some effective synthesis or middle ground of "realism" and violence. I might be reading you wrong. Am I? This is why I need your contribution for my deeper understanding and for our conversation. See you on Jan. 30.

Best, Ira

From Bill Holmes, February 1, 2002

Dear Ira,

Please allow me a footnote to our dialogue, lest I misrepresent my mentor, Reinhold Niebuhr. At the end of our Wednesday session, you asked me if I thought Niebuhr believed that love (or peace) would eventually triumph in history. I think I answered "probably not." Riding home, I remembered a Niebuhr book in my library, entitled "Beyond Tragedy." It's a series of essays on the question you posed. In the Preface he insists "… the center, source, and fulfillment of history lie beyond history… It is the thesis of these essays that the Christian view of history… is tragic insofar as it recognizes evil as an inevitable concomitant of even the highest spiritual enterprises. It is beyond tragedy insofar as it does not regard evil as inherent in existence itself but as finally under the dominion of a good God." [149] I just wanted to be clear that I think Niebuhr's "pessimism" about human history is grounded in his understanding of our sinfulness, and that even that sin is finally overcome by God's grace and forgiveness.

While I'm writing, the other thing I did when I got home was read two articles that Jerry Weiss copied from "First Things" and brought to me. One was the Dec. 2001 article by the editors, entitled "In a Time of War." Accompanying it were the Feb. 2002 response by Stanley Hauerwas, and the editors' response to Hauerwas. It's good to know that "our dialogue" is going on today in lots of places. [150]

But the one that really grabbed me was the Feb. 2002 article, "The Continuing Irony of American History," by Wilfred M. McClay. Have you read it? He says everything I've been trying to say - but so much better. And his knowledge of Niebuhr far exceeds my own. He only jumped the track in one place. While I think he is right to warn that abortion, euthanasia, physician-assisted suicide, and stem-cell experimentation can lead to a "medical and biotechnological degradation of human life," he stops being Niebuhrian by failing to also allow for the humanitarian values that can be derived from these practices as well. I believe Niebuhr would find the potential for both promise and tragedy in all of these examples - depending on how they were applied and for what reason.

Damn! This "footnote" has become an epistle! Sorry

about its length. I'll close by saying I'm entirely converted to "First Things" and will be sending off my subscription pronto.

Stay well. You are a "means of grace" to more of us than you know - even when we disagree.

Bill

From Ira Zepp, February 1, 2002

Dear Bill,

Actually, the "first thing" I do with a new book is go to the footnotes and endnotes; they are often more interesting and insightful than the text. Thanks for yours! Re: Niebuhr's "fulfillment of history lies beyond history" - I think MLK, Yoder, etc. Might say, "Okay, but let's work as hard as we can to approximate in history what lies beyond it; live more eschatologically, as they say."

Or, to paraphrase Bonhoeffer, what is beyond tragedy is also in the midst of tragedy, working its way through historical contradictions and ambiguity toward a fuller and richer humanity. I know how utterly foolish this sounds, given 9/11, and yet that foolishness may be wiser than we might think. I have subscribed to *First Things* since the mid-nineties and am fascinated by it - fascinated in the sense I mentioned the other day - I can't stay away from it and am repelled and disgusted by it at the same time. It is theologically sophisticated, well-written and rationally argued, sometimes too contentious (especially the Richard Neuhaus stuff), often maddening, but always provocative and beneficial for a romantic like me, and that is why I like it.

I always like to read the other side; it has been, in a "realistic" way, my reality check. As I mentioned earlier, that Quaker community I knew as a child, Martin King, Gandhi, others in that tradition, and to some degree now, Hauerwas (although I disagree with a lot of other things he says) keep me what I think I've always been - a romantic (not a liberal!) out of which comes a hope, possibility, and capacity for change, if not revolutions.

Thank God, you're around to be my reality check. You are a prince. Hang in there with the compassion that underpins the world.

Ira

Conclusion - Bill Holmes

Dear Ira,

Your generous invitation to write the conclusion to our email dialogue causes me to recall a note that Robert McAfee Brown once put at the top of a paper I wrote in a class at Union Theological Seminary. The paper was on John Wesley's concept of Christians' "going on to perfection." The gist of the paper was that Wesley never envisioned arriving at a perfect state in this world, but that Christians are under an imperative to strive and keep progressing (a mandate reflected, I think, more in your point of view than mine). While giving the paper a decent grade, Professor Brown wrote in the upper-right hand corner, "I'm almost persuaded - but not quite."

That's exactly how I feel about our dialogue. In many ways, I've moved closer to your perspective on the power and promise of nonviolence. At the same time, in other ways, our dialogue has helped me clarify the reasons I cannot, in most instances, hold the pacifist position. "I'm almost persuaded - but not quite!"

The best quote of all, however, is from Reinhold Niebuhr. It represents an attitude that both of us try to practice, and that has made possible our lively, but mutually respectful exchange: "We must each be willing to see the truth in our opponent's error and the error in our own truth." [151] I'm grateful for the journey we have made together into that kind of effort.

Bill

About the Authors

CHARLES E. COLLYER - Charles Collyer received his doctorate in Psychology from Princeton University in 1976. A professor at the University of Rhode Island for forty years, he was the recipient of several awards for his teaching, and twice served as chair of the Psychology Department. He was a co-founder of the Center for Nonviolence and Peace Studies at URI. With Dr. Pamela Zappardino, he co-directs The Ira and Mary Zepp Center for Nonviolence and Peace Education, a program of the traditional arts organization Common Ground on the Hill, in Westminster MD. Please visit the Center's web page www.commongroundonthehill.org/zeppcenter.html. The Zepp Center offers workshops and consultation on nonviolent problem-solving for organizations and groups of all kinds. Email address: zeppcenter@gmail.com. Charlie's author page is www.tryforfurther.com.

IRA G. ZEPP, JR. - The late Ira Zepp (1929-2009) received his doctorate from St. Mary's Seminary and University, and did graduate work in Islam at Hartford Theological Seminary. He studied in India, Mexico, Israel, and Eastern Europe. For 31 years he taught religious studies at McDaniel College (formerly Western Maryland College), and the College's principal teaching award is named for him. A social gospel advocate, he encouraged young people to become involved in the Civil Rights Movement and to work for social justice. He is remembered for saying "To know and not to act, is not to know." He authored many articles and 12 books, two of which are about the thought of Martin Luther King, Jr.

WILLIAM A. HOLMES - For 24 years Bill Holmes was the Senior Minister at Metropolitan Memorial, the National Methodist Church in Washington DC. Before that, he served campus-related churches in Dallas, Denton, and Austin, Texas. He is a graduate of Perkins School of Theology, and did post-graduate work at Union Theological Seminary in New York, where he studied with Reinhold Niebuhr and Paul Tillich. He has served as the Chairman of the Ethics Advisory Committee at Sibley Memorial Hospital in Washington DC.

BERNARD LAFAYETTE, JR. - Bernard LaFayette, the author of the Foreword to *Nonviolence: Origins and Outcomes*, was a Freedom Rider and served as a member of Martin Luther King's executive staff during the U.S. Civil Rights Movement. He has been a prominent nonviolence educator ever since Dr. King's assassination. A Harvard University Ed.D., he is a former President of his alma mater, American Baptist College in Nashville, Tennessee. He served as Director of the Center for Nonviolence and Peace Studies at the University of Rhode Island, and as Distinguished Scholar in Residence at Emory University. He currently teaches at Auburn University, near his home in Tuskegee, Alabama, and serves as Chair of the Southern Christian Leadership Conference and of the International Nonviolence Conference Board.

Endnotes

[1] For examples, see A Force More Powerful, the Public Broadcasting System's series of six short documentaries on successful nonviolent movements for social and political change in India, the United States, Poland, South Africa, Chile, and Denmark. The book of the same name contains chapters on these and several more international examples of nonviolence at work.

[2] For a readable treatment of alternative theories of anger, see Carol Tavris's book Anger: The Misunderstood Emotion (Simon & Schuster).

[3] Some will point out that the Golden Rule is only conditionally nonviolent, because it assumes that a person wants to be treated well. In the case of a person who wishes harm or destruction upon him- or herself, its usefulness as a nonviolent guideline dissolves. For example, in "suicide by police," a person violently attacks police officers because he wants the officers to kill him. However, in this section we ask readers to assume the standard interpretation of the Golden Rule. We should also note that multicultural educators, including our colleague Dr. Pamela Zappardino, prefer a revised, less ego-centric "Platinum Rule," which might be phrased "Treat others as they prefer to be treated." This rule is proactive, giving a guideline for our behavior in advance of knowing what others' behavior will be.

[4] For an excellent treatment of violence from this perspective, see Aaron T. Beck's Prisoners of Hate: The Cognitive Basis of Anger, Hostility, and Violence (Harper Collins).

[5] James Gilligan, M.D., an experienced prison psychiatrist and author of Violence: Reflections on a National Epidemic (Vintage), proposes that all violence is rooted in shame, or disrespect. Gilligan further proposes that love, guilt, fear, and knowledge of alternatives, can serve as brakes on the violence that is triggered by shame. By implication, the occurrence of violence suggests that these brakes did not work.

[6] The extent to which governments seem to discount the significance of collateral damage when they go to war appalls peace advocates and often radicalizes noncombatants. An important challenge for students of nonviolence is to become more effective at pressing this issue, drawing attention to the unintended consequences of the very neglect of unintended consequences!

[7] Our textbook in this course was Psychology in Perspective, by Tavris and Wade. The five broad perspectives on Psychology presented in this text are: Biological, Learning, Cognitive, and Psychodynamic.

[8] A Force More Powerful is a video series consisting of six short documentaries on nonviolence-inspired movements for social change. A book of the same title by Ackerman and Duvall recounts these and other stories of nonviolence from the 20th Century.

[9] A compact review of several of these is given in Sharon Erickson Nepstad's book Nonviolent Revolutions: Civil Resistance in the Late 20th Century (Oxford, 2011).

[10] The Children, by David Halberstam (Random House, 1998) tells the story of the Nashville sit-in movement through the lives of eight of the young students who led the campaign, one of whom was Bernard LaFayette Jr. The book goes on to trace the involvement of several of these "children" in subsequent events of the Civil Rights Movement, and continues their stories up to the late 1990s. A table of contents for The Children is included in the Kindle e-book A Look Inside David Halberstam's The Children, authored by one of us (Charlie).

[11] Stanley Milgram was a psychologist who became famous for an experiment on obedience to authority. In this experiment, human subjects, who had been told that they were assisting in research on learning, were instructed to deliver ostensibly painful shocks to another person (who was actually an actor). Surprisingly, many subjects continued to obey by increasing the shock level, even when the shocks were apparently causing injury. The study raised questions of many

kinds, but at minimum showed that direct instructions from a person in authority have a powerful influence on behavior.

[12] Tough Guise, a hard-hitting documentary about violence and male socialization by Jackson Katz, was another video seen by this class during the same semester.

[13] Philip Zimbardo, another psychologist, showed that even arbitrarily assigned roles can also strongly shape behavior. In his "prison study" some students played the role of guards and others the role of prisoners in a mock prison. In an account that has become legend in the field of psychology, the study was terminated early because the "guards" went beyond guarding, and began to exhibit cruel and abusive behavior toward their "prisoners."

[14] Walter Wink, a U.S. theologian, uses the term third way to refer to nonviolence as seen in the teachings of Jesus. The first way of responding to an offense or threat would be passivity, or flight. The second would be violent retaliation, or fighting. Nonviolence is a third, more creative alternative in which the opponent and the conflict are engaged deliberately and respectfully. See, for example, Wink's 1998 book The Powers That Be: Theology for a New Millenium, published by Galilee/Doubleday.

[15] A curriculum source book for this approach is the "Leader's Manual": LaFayette, Jr., B., & Jehnsen, D.C. (1995) The Leader's Manual: A structured guide and introduction to Kingian nonviolence: The philosophy and methodology. Galena, OH: Institute for Human Rights and Responsibilities.

[16] Solzhenitsyn, A. (1992) The Gulag Archipelago: 1918-1956. An Experiment in Literary Investigation. Vol. III. New York: Harper/Collins, p. 615.

[17] Ury, W. (1999) Getting to Peace: Transforming Conflict at Home, at work, and in the World. New York: Viking.

[18] King, Jr., M.L. (1963) Strength to Love. Philadelphia: Fortress Press.

[19] Cohen, J.R. & Fiffer, S. (Eds.) (1989). Free at Last: A History of the Civil Rights Movement and Those Who Died in the Struggle. Montgomery AL: Teaching Tolerance.

[20] King, Jr., M. L. (1958). Stride Toward Freedom: The Montgomery Story. San Francisco: Harper.

[21] A more detailed account of this history and of the principles of nonviolence is available in Ira Zepp's work on the Pilgrimage chapter: Smith, K.L. & Zepp, Jr., I.G. (1998) Search for the Beloved Community. Valley Forge PA: Judson; and Zepp, Jr., I.G. (1971) The Social Vision of Martin Luther King, Jr. New York: Carlson.

[22] Gilligan, J. (1996) Violence: Reflections on a National Epidemic. New York: Vintage Books.

[23] Martin Luther King was acutely aware that personal animosities continually threatened both his supporters and those who opposed him. He repeatedly sought a detached and firm but courteous way of prodding both sides to address the issues rather than insulting and spitefully undermining each other.

[24] King, Jr., M. L. (1963) Letter from Birmingham Jail. Chapter 5 (pp. 77-100) in Why We Can't Wait. New York: Harper & Row, p.79.

[25] Daniel Kahneman has drawn attention to the distinction between these two kinds of human cognition in his book Thinking, Fast and Slow (2011) New York: Farrar, Strous and Giroux.

[26] King, Jr., M. L. (1963). Why We Can't Wait. New York: Harper & Row.

[27] Film footage capturing this moment is included in the segment of the video series A Force More Powerful that tells the Nashville story. The segment is title We Were Warriors.

[28] Fisher, R., Ury, W. & Patton, B. (1991) Getting to Yes: Negotiating Agreement Without Giving In. 2nd ed. New York: Penguin.

[29] King, Jr., M. L. (1963) Why We Can't Wait, p. 79. (Letter from Birmingham Jail).

[30] For example, in current conflicts between the police and youth of color in cities all across the United States, both sides have a "bad apple" problem. That is, the vast majority of police are not trigger-happy, though a few bad apples could be described that way. Likewise, the vast majority of youth are not thugs, although the behavior of a few might lead some people to use that term. Both police and youth are therefore stereotyped in a shallow and misleading, but similar, way. What if this became their common ground? What if a reconciliation is possible in which police use their authority to advocate for the needs of the youth rather than to merely control their behavior through force?

[31] Here is a link to the text of Thoreau's essay:
http://xroads.virginia.edu/~hyper2/thoreau/civil.html

[32] Tolstoy's views are forcefully presented in his book The Kingdom of God is Within You.

[33] For examples, see Chacham, R. (2003), Breaking Ranks: Refusing to Serve in the West Bank and Gaza Strip, New York: Other Press; and Laufer, P. (2006), Mission Rejected: U.S. Soldiers Who Say No to Iraq, White River Junction: Chelsea Green.

[34] Halberstam, D. (1998). The Children. New York, Fawcett, pp. 137-138. See also Collyer, C. E. (2015). A Look Inside David Halberstam's The Children. Kindle ebook.

[35] From Arun Gandhi's pamphlet M. K. Gandhi's Wit and Wisdom, p. 40 (no date). Memphis TN: Gandhi Institute.

[36] From the article Love, law and civil disobedience, in New South, vol. 16, Dec. 1961; quoted in Smith, K. & Zepp Jr., I. G. (1974), Search for the Beloved Community: The thinking of Martin Luther King, Jr. Valley Forge: Judson.

[37] From the Letter from Birmingham Jail, in MLK's 1963 book Why We Can't Wait, New York: Harper & Row, p. 98.

[38] From Reinhold Niebuhr, Moral Man and Immoral Society (1932), New York: Scribner's, p. 246.

[39] ibid., p. 250.

[40] ibid., p. 252.

[41] From the Letter from Birmingham Jail, in MLK's book Why We Can't Wait (1963), p. 81.

[42] We are grateful to our colleague Frank Gallo for acquainting us with aikido. Frank is a former police officer, a nonviolence trainer, and an aikido master.

[43] Bandura, A., Ross, D., and Ross, S. A. (1961). Transmission of aggression through imitation of aggressive models. Journal of Abnormal and Social Psychology, 63, 575-582.

[44] Johnson, D. W. And Johnson, R. T. (1996). Conflict resolution and peer mediation programs in elementary and secondary schools: A review of the research. Review of Educational Research, Winter 1996, 66, No. 4, 459-506.

[45] Goleman, D. Emotional Intelligence: Why It Can Matter More Than IQ. New York: Bantam, 1995.

[46] Hallak, M. "Nonviolence training program evaluation" (2001). Dissertations and Master's Theses. Paper AAI3025568. http://digitalcommons.uri.edu/dissertations/AAI3025568

[47] Collyer, C. E., Johnson, K. L, de Mesquita, P. B., Palazzo, L. A., & Jordan, D. (2010). Sensitivity to violence measured by ratings of severity increases after nonviolence training. Perceptual & Motor Skills, 110(1), 48-60.

[48] Collyer, C. E., Gallo, F. J., Corey, J., Waters, D., & Boney-McCoy, S. (2007). Typology of violence derived from ratings of severity and provocation. Perceptual & Motor Skills, 104(2), 637-653.

[49] Collyer, C. E., Brell, A., Moster, A., & Furey, J. (2011). Individual differences in sensitivity to violence. Perceptual & Motor Skills, 113(3), 703-714.

[50] Lipsey, M. W. & Wilson, D. B. (1993). The efficacy of psychological, educational, and behavioral treatment: Confirmation from meta-analysis. American Psychologist, 48, 1181-1209.

[51] Durlak, J. A., Weissberg, R. P., Dymnicki, A. B., Taylor, R. D. & Schellinger, K. B. (2011). The impact of enhancing students' social and emotional learning: A meta-analysis of school-based universal interventions. Child Development, 82(1): 405–432.

[52] Duckworth, A. (2016). Don't grade schools on Grit. New York Times, March 26, 2016.

[53] The description of Just War Theory paraphrases Paul Robinson's in his article titled "Ready to kill but not to die: NATO strategy in Kosovo," International Journal, Autumn 1999.

[54] "Send in a thousand grandmothers" is the first line of the song 1000 Grandmothers, by singer and activist Holly Near.

[55] Nepstad, S. (2011). Nonviolent Revolutions: Civil Resistance in the Late 20th Century (Oxford, 2011).

[56] All of the quotations are from the 1952 Revised Standard Version of the Bible.

[57] For an extended discussion, see Nygren, Anders, *Agape and Eros*, New York, Harper Torch Books, 1953, pp. 75-81.

[58] *Agape and Eros*, p. 210. There has been a good deal of criticism of this comparison as simplistic and reductionist. *Philia*, another Greek word for love, having to do with reciprocity in human relations, mutuality in friendship, and neighborly companionship, is often used as a mediating link between *eros* and *agape*. Martin Luther King Jr. often made use of this trifurcation of love in his sermons and essays to defend the notion that *agape* is a viable force for nonviolence. Nevertheless, with this comparison Nygren helps us see what Christianity claims to be the

285

unique essence of God. While being holy and wrathful, God is not finally that; God is finally love. For a more systematic critique of Nygren, see Outak, Gene, *Agape: An Ethical Analysis*, New Haven and London, Yale University Press, 1973, and for two scholarly reviews of Outak's book, see Erling, Berhhard (pp. 25-29) and Graber, Glenn C. (pp. 29-34), *Agape*: An Ethical Analysis. *Religious Studies Review*, vol. 1, Sept 1975.

[59] II Corinthians 5:19.

[60] See Aulen, Gustav, *Christus Victor*, London, SPCK, 1953, pp. 162-167.

[61] From "Love, Law, and Civil Disobedience," in *A Testament of Hope: The Essential Writings of Martin Luther King, Jr.*, edited by James Washington, Harper & Row, San Francisco, 1986, pp. 46-47.

[62] *Sojourners,* Nov. 1986, p. 15. Sojourners published a series of four articles by Wink from Nov. 1986 to Feb. 1987 on the subject of nonviolent resistance to evil.

[63] *Matthew 5:38-41.* We are indebted to Wink for his exegetical insights into these verses. See also *Matthew 5:44-45,* "You have heard that it was said, 'You shall love your neighbor and hate your enemy. But I say to you, love your enemies and pray for those who persecute you." It is obvious that this *agapaic* love for enemies is the foundation for forgiving them, as expressed in the actions of turning the other cheek, or going the second mile. It is apparent that Wink does not feel that these "hard teachings" of Jesus are the "interim ethic" of Albert Schweitzer or the "counsel of perfection" of Roman Catholic monasticism or the "impossible possibility" of Reinhold Niebuhr. Wink, along with Martin Luther King and Gandhi, takes these words of Jesus as practical and possible guidelines for Christian living.

[64] *Sojourners,* Dec. 1986, p. 29.

[65] *Sojourners*, Dec. 1986, p. 29 and *Sojourners*, Nov. 1986, p. 15. See also the conclusion of the apostle Paul's summary of the Sermon on the Mount (especially *Matthew 5*), in *Romans* 12:21. "Do not be overcome by evil, but overcome evil with good."

[66] Martin Luther King, Jr., *Strength to Love*. Philadelphia, Fortress Press, 1981, pp 50-51.

[67] Jones, L. Gregory, *Embodying Forgiveness: A Theological Analysis.* Grand Rapids, Eerdmans Publishing, 1995, p. 66. See also pp 195-196.

[68] Volf, Miroslav, *Exclusion and Embrace: A Theological Exploration of Identity, Otherness, and Reconciliation.* Nashville, Abington Press, 1996, pp 275-306.

[69] Niebuhr, Reinhold, *The Nature and Destiny of Man: A Christian Interpretation.* Gifford Lectures. New York: Charles Scribner's Sons, 1953. Vol. II (Human Destiny), p. 246. See also Vol. I (Human Nature), p. 285. Niebuhr's treatment of love and justice is discussed in Zepp Jr., Ira G., *The Social Vision of Martin Luther King, Jr.,* Brooklyn, Carlson Publishing, 1989, pp. 148-150.

[70] Martin Luther King, Jr., *Where Do We Go From Here: Chaos or Community?* New York, Harper & Row, 1967, pp. 89-90.

[71] *Ibid.*, p. 37.

[72] See *The Baltimore Sun*, "Score One for Friendship," by Ken Rosenthal, Oct 17 1999, p. 56. See also the July 8 2013 Sports Illustrated Vault article "Roberto Alomar & John Hirschbeck," by Albert Chen:

[73] http://www.si.com/vault/2015/07/09/106342560/roberto-alomar--john-hirschbeck

[74] This section is adapted from Ferguson, John, *The Politics of Love: The New Testament and Nonviolent Revolution.* New York: Fellowship Publications, 1979, pp 105-106.

[75] Peter Storey in "A Different Kind of Justice: Truth and Reconciliation in south Africa," in *The Christian Century*, Sept 10-17, 1997, p. 788. We have excerpted two paragraphs from Storey's article to give a sense of the TRC's impact on South Africa and the world. An appreciative, yet critical, perspective on the TRC is found in a review by Sara Ruden of Desmond Tutu's book, *No Future Without Forgiveness,* in *The Christian Century,* July 5-12, 2000, pp. 722-725.

[76] See the Toronto Star's summary of these recommentations: https://www.thestar.com/news/canada/2015/06/02/highlights-of-truth-and-reconciliation-commissions-recommendations-on-residential-

schools.html

[77] Gregg, Richard, *The Power of Nonviolence*, 2nd Revised Edition, New York: Schocken Books, 1966. See especially pp 43-46.

[78] King Jr., M. L., *Why We Can't Wait*, New York: Harper & Row, 1963, pp. 107-108.

[79] Eliade, Mircea, *Patanjali and Yoga*, New York: Schocken Books, 1975, p. 63.

[80] Although Jainism emphasizes *ahimsa* as its greatest virtue, warfare and militarism were legitimized and accepted by many Jains and most Indians. Compare Christianity's history of sponsoring wars and crusades, and its wrestling with the theory of just war, while proclaiming as its core message, "peace on earth and good will toward all." What Ronald Goetz has said of Christians might also be applied to Jainism: "Whenever Christians engage in coercion in the name of their faith and dogma, their actions somehow seem more reprehensible than those of other people doing the same thing. Christians should realize that whenever they engage in violence in the name of the persecuted Christ, they directly deny Christ. The world has every right to expect and to demand that Christians, who talk as good a love game as anyone, act in a manner consistent with their rhetoric. This is why anti-Christians get so much mileage out of the long history of Christian violence against its foes or its 'heretics'." (*Christian Century*, July 16-23, 1997, p. 653.

[81] This version of the vows is from Van Voorst, Robert E., *Anthology of World Scriptures*, Belmont CA, 1994, p. 115. The commentary is ours.

[82] Gandhi, M. K. *Non-Violent Resistance*, New York: Schocken Books, 1968, pp. 41-42.

[83] For a more detailed discussion, read Noss, John and Noss, David, *Man's Religions*, 7th ed., New York: MacMillan, 1989, pp. 99-107.

[84] Ferguson, John, *War and Peace in the World's Religions*, New York: Oxford University Press, 1978, p. 34.

[85] Huston Smith interprets these aspects of Buddhism very well in *The World's Religions*, San Francisco, Harper, 1991, pp. 99-112.

[86] This translation is from Lal, P. *Bhagavad Gita*, Calcutta: Writers Workshop, 1965.

[87] Gandhi, M., *The Law of Love*, edited by Anand T. Hingori, Bombay, Gharatji Vidya, Bhavan, 1062, p. 1. (Hereafter referred to as LL). To support this thesis further, Gandhi said "Truth, harmony, brotherhood, and justice are attributes of *ahimsa*." LL, p. 7.

[88] LL, p. 3. Also, "*Ahimsa* is a science. The word 'failure' has no place in the vocabulary of science. Failure to obtain the expected result is often the precursor to further discoveries." LL, p. 81.

[89] He often refers to "God" in his prayers and conversations. Although *Isvara*, a word for a personal dimension of Brahman, was available to Gandhi, some say his use of "God" was a way to help westerners gain access to his spiritual discourse. He interchangeably used Hindu and Christian concepts of the supreme Being, and it is Gandhi himself who sees love, *ahimsa*, nonviolence, and truth as compatible terms. One even sees this compatibility in indices of books about Gandhi. See Chatterjee, Margaret, *Gandhi's Religious Thought*, Notre Dame Indiana, University of Notre Dame Press, 1983, and Ashe, Geoffrey, *Gandhi*, New York: Stein and Day, 1972.

[90] Non-Violent Resistance, *op. cit.*, p. 21.

[91] From Harijan, April 15, 1933

[92] LL, p. 70.

[93] Gandhi, M.K. *Autobiography*, part IV, chap. 26.

[94] Prabhu, R. & Rao, U., eds, *The Mind of Mahatma Gandhi, Rev. Ed.* Ahemadabad, 1967.

[95] Quoted in Bondurant, J., *The Conquest of Violence: The Gandhian Philosophy of Conflict. Berkeley: University of California, 1967, p.19. Recall Arjuna's statement in the Gita: "The untrue never is; the True never isn't; the knower of Truth knows this."*

[96] See Bondurant, *op. cit.*, p. 9.

[97] Non-Violent Resistance, *op. cit.*, pp. 251-252.

[98] LL, p. 40. See also "*Ahimsa* is not merely non-killing. A person who remains smugly satisfied with the non-killing of noxious life, but has not love in his heart for all that lives, will be counted as least in the Kingdom of Heaven." LL, p. 45.

[99] Gandhi, M., *All Men Are Brothers: Autobiographical Reflections.* New York: Continuum, 1984, p. 74.

[100] LL, p. 38.

[101] *Non-Violent Resistance, op. cit.*, p. 42.

[102] Harak, G. S., ed., *Nonviolence for the Third Millenium.* Macon GA: Mercer University Press, 2000, p. 121.

[103] LL, p. 14.

[104] LL, p. 54.

[105] LL, p. 55. See also LL, pp 56, 58, 93-94, and *All Men Are Brothers, op. cit.*, pp 92-97.

[106] *Non-Violent Resistance, op. cit.*, p. 52.

[107] *Ibid.*, p. 132. The "but" is a crucial qualifier pointing to Walter Wink's "third way" -- nonviolence as the alternative to both violence and passivity.

[108] *Non-Violent Resistance, op. cit.*, p. 364. See also pp 95, 189, and 252.

[109] *All Men are Brothers, op. cit.*, p. 82.

[110] LL, pp. 63-64.

[111] LL, p. 79.

[112] Gandhi, M., *Autobiography: The Story of My Experiments With Truth.* Boston: Beacon Press, 1969, p. Xiii.

[113] LL, p. 37. See also pp 39-40

[114] *Non-Violent Resistance, op. cit.*, p. 132.

[115] *All Men Are Brothers, op. cit.*, pp 83-84. One wonders why Gandhi did not consider Hitler, whom he thought could be converted by dedicated

satyagrahis, a lunatic running amuck in Europe. For Gandhi's reflections on this, see NVR, p. 348ff.

[116] *Autobiography, op. cit.*, p. 469.

[117] *Non-Violent Resistance, op. cit.*, p. 56.

[118] New York: Hill and Wang, 1967. The quotations here are from pp 106-107.

[119] Thich Nhat Nanh. "In Search of the Enemy of Man (addressed to (the Rev.) Martin Luther King)." In Nhat Nanh, Ho Huu Tuong, Tam Ich, Bui Giang, Pham Cong Thien. *Dialogue.* Saigon: La Boi, 1965. P. 11-20.

[120] For a complete schedule of and rationale for this event, see Bondurant, pp 46-52.

[121] *All Men are Brothers, op. cit.*, p. 120.

[122] *Nonviolence for the Third Millenium, op. cit.*, p. 186.

[123] *Ibid.* p. 188.

[124] Johnson, D. And Johnson, R. Conflict resolution and peer mediation programs in elementary and secondary schools: A review of the research. *Review of Educational Research,* Winter 1996, 66, No. 4, 459-506. This well-known review is representative of a growing body of evidence on the value of instruction on conflict management for both social and academic development.

[125] *Non-Violent Resistance, op. cit.*, p. 109.

[126] LL, p. 66. It is instructive to note that, for traditional Christianity, *agape* is a derivative value; that is, we do not have it by virtue of birth; it is bestowed by God. *Ahimsa*, on the other hand, is an inherent value - part of our makeup because we are extensions of *Brahman*.

[127] LL, p. 35.

[128] Martin Luther King Jr., "The ethical demands for integration." *Religion and Labor*, Vol. VI, No. 8 (May, 1963), p. 4.

[129] Martin Luther King Jr., *Trumpet of Conscience*, New York: Harper &

Row, 1968, p. 69.

[130] LL, p. 99. Many critics consider this naive, romantic, and optimistic view of humanity the Achilles heel of nonviolent movements. Dietrich Bonhoeffer, once an ardent pacifist, was a member of a team that planned to assassinate Hitler. Bonhoeffer's basic position was that tyranny itself was worse than the violence of assassinating a tyrant. As we have discussed, there are few pure nonviolent resisters.

[131] *Nonviolent Resistance, op. cit.*, pp. 12-14 and 350-352.

[132] See Chapter 6 in King's *Stride Toward Freedom* for a version of Pilgrimage to Nonviolence that includes all six of his principles of nonviolence.

[133] For an excellent discussion of how dependent King was on these liberal resources, see Keith D. Miller's *Voice of Deliverance: The Language of Martin Luther King Jr. And its Sources*, New York: The Free Press (Macmillan), 1992.

[134] Little, D. (2000). Coming to Terms with Religious Militancy. *Harvard Divinity Bulletin, 29,* (1), 19.

[135] See also the related article "SCLC president joins forces with Gorbachev in peace effort." The Louisiana Weekly, Nov. 24, 2014

[136] http://www.louisianaweekly.com/sclc-president-joins-forces-with-gorbachev-in-peace-effort/.

[137] The book *Nonviolent Revolutions,* by Sharon Erickson Nepstad (Oxford University Press, 2011) examines six nonviolent revolutions - three successful (East Germany, Chile, and the Philippines) and three unsuccessful (Tiananmen Square, Panama, and Kenya) - in an effort to identify factors responsible for success and failure. In each of the successful cases, including the former Soviet satellite East Germany, a nonviolent popular movement grew first, and then was joined by elements of the military and government authorities.

[138] Reinhold Niebuhr, 1940, quoted by E. J. Dionne, Jr., "Pacifists, Serious and Otherwise," Washington Post, October 29, 2001.

[139] *Report of the U.S. Conference of Bishops*, November 18, 2001.

[140] Hollander, P. (2001), "It's a crime that some don't see this as hate." Washington Post, October 21, 2001.

[141] Buchanan, J. M. (2001), Oil dependents. Editorial, *The Christian Century*, December 5.

[142] A group founded by Robert Funk of the Westar Institute.

[143] Methodist Youth Fellowship

[144] Trollinger, W. V. (2001), Nonviolent voices. *The Christian Century*, December 12.

[145] An abridged version of Bill Holmes's position paper appeared in the January 2, 2002 *UM Connection*, a newspaper published bi-weekly by the Baltimore-Washington Conference of the United Methodist Church.

[146] Isaiah 10:5,6

[147] Niebuhr, Reinhold (1932, 1960), *Moral Man and Immoral Society*. New York: Charles Scribner's Sons.

[148] Macdonald, M. (2002) Caught in the middle. *The Christian Century*, January 2.

[149] Niebuhr, Reinhold (1937), Beyond tragedy. New York: Scribner, pp *ix to xi*.

[150] *First Things* is a neo-conservative journal dedicated to the discussion of religion and public policy. Its editor at the time of this writing was Richard John Neuhaus.

[151] Reinhold Niebuhr, quoted by E. J. Dionne, Jr., *Harvard Divinity School Bulletin*, Winter, 2001-2002.

VISIT CHARLES COLLYER'S AUTHOR PAGE ON

WWW.AMAZON.COM

AND HIS WEBSITE AT

WWW.TRYFORFURTHER.COM.

CPSIA information can be obtained
at www.ICGtesting.com
Printed in the USA
BVHW040220240119
538573BV00022B/267/P

9 781978 395886